ENGLAND
LOST AND FOUND

England Lost and Found *is a lively attempt to understand the nature of England and its people by a mature writer, travelling on foot and by bicycle, falling off, taking wrong turns, being apprehended by the police . . . but, in the end, like King Alfred his hero, winning through.*

NOTE:
The riches of Cambridge, Ely and the broader reaches of East Anglia – with more respect for Kings Lynn – are reserved for a further volume.

Front Cover Illustration shows King Alfred standing tall and proud in the town square in Wantage.

ENGLAND
LOST AND FOUND

by

PETER DAVIES

THE EARTHLING PRESS

ENGLAND LOST AND FOUND
by Peter Davies

ISBN 0 9551526-0-7
ISBN 978-0-9551526-0-3

British Library Cataloguing in Publication Data
A catalogue record for this book is available from the British Library

Printed and Bound in Great Britain by
Woolnough Bookbinding Ltd
Irthlingborough, Northants

CONTENTS

DEDICATION

To Jean, who puts up with me and my absences.

FOREWORD

by Ronald Blythe

THIS is an enchanting travel book. Peter Davies takes us to where shelves-full of county guides have taken us, but so differently. It is his pace – that set by walking and by a Concept mountain-bike, not the car. "Walking promotes thought; cycling propels ideas", he says, and here is evidence of these truths. He carries the minimum of luggage with him but a long lifetime of learning. The distinctive youthfulness of the retired schoolmaster, which is a kind of professional hazard, causing aged men to explore like boys, is apparent throughout, and our familiar country is seen all afresh. Although we know its main history and geography, reflected by this traveller, it loses its popular image and becomes a personal land which the reader is invited to share, and thus somewhere he has never been before. This is the art of the traveller's tale.

These are English journeys which stop at the borders because, as Peter Davies confesses, journeys have to come to an end somewhere. But they allow him to meditate on his own Englishness en-route. It is a book written on the hoof and in the (bicycle) saddle, and it moves along with just the right kind of momentum for seeing and noting the small as well as the great sights. There are beautifully informed accounts of farming, woodland, birds and wild flowers. Churches and cathedrals are always visited and, what is more, worshipped in, B and Bs and pubs are given Davies ratings, and there is all the way that 'caught' snatch of talk which is the genius of every good traveller from William Cobbett to Bruce Chatwyn. Although very much alone, Peter Davies is not a loner. He is a sociable Englishman sharing his vision of a world which exists between the new motorways, a still-marvellous landscape which carries the shaping of centuries and where people of all ages have not been entirely flattened out by pop culture, but show their regional origins still. His hero is Alfred the Great, the founder of England – and its first English teacher. All the same, this is not an essay on patriotism but a successful attempt to pass on an extraordinary private happiness as the miles are slowly eaten up and the rain comes down and the sun shines, and the old and new houses look up from their seasonal gardens, and the animals from their pastures. It is all there, Davies is telling us, for anyone to see, though not from a car.

England Lost and Found is a delightful exploration in the tradition of W.H. Hudson, Edward Thomas and land-trampers of authority with an eye and an ear for whatever happens to be passing, travellers on the home ground who are there to remind us of its quiet existence and its unexpected excitements.

The Building Blocks of England

Melverley Church, Shropshire, sits on one bank of the Severn, its rock-like timbers of English oak still withstanding the ravages of time and tide.

Alfred the Great
The West Saxon King
Born at Wantage A.D. 849

Alfred found learning dead
and restored it
Education neglected
And revived it
The laws powerless
and he gave them force
The Church debased
and he raised it
The land ravaged by a fearful enemy
from which he delivered it.
Alfred's name will live
as long as mankind
shall respect the past.

Inscription on Alfred's statue at Wantage

Beverley to my mind perfectly represents Alfred's vision of England, 'lost' though it was as yet to him; and a pinch of its airy grace is seen dimly in Titanium secured to the railings below.

airy strength and grace

TO THE READER

THE journeys about England described in this book were mostly made by bicycle or on foot. They were not planned. There was no particular timetable. I did not have a watch. Sometimes I took a map and lost it. (One blew out of my trouser pocket at night on the A12 when I was trying to avoid going to Ipswich.)

Somewhere back in my childhood I had seen maps of England, indiscriminately coloured as school maps sometimes were, and I knew about King Alfred's Wessex, Offa's Mercia and Bede's Northumbria. There were also large areas infested by Danes. These were the main building blocks. I would use them.

'Why only England'?' you may ask. 'Why only anywhere?' There had to be a limit. At my age, I couldn't take on the world.

'Why lost'?' The word has so many meanings. It may only mean missed – as in the road or turn not taken – or it may mean mislaid. 'Lost?' I hear my mother cry, aiming her automatic machine gun at me. 'Then find it!' And in the finding, as we well know from the parable of the lost coin, is all the joy. Of course, lost may also mean mined or eroded beyond repair, the sea being not the only agent not willing always to give back with one hand what it has taken away with the other.

I have taken Alfred the Great as my hero, he being the first to realise that England could not be built by force alone and the first to understand the value of negotiation. The great thing about Alfred is that no matter which way the coin came down he made the most of it.

Amid all the fashionable talk about conservation, how many people stop to wonder who or what saved England in the past? After Alfred, Nelson and Churchill spring to mind. But even Churchill in the twentieth century

1

would not have paid much attention to words like conservation and environment. His contemporaries talked of the country, not the country-side. Somewhere under all our present day anxiety about the future of England lies the suspicion that our country has a naturally robust ability to regenerate itself.

'Is it safe? You might be knocked off and left for dead in a ditch! Have you got a helmet? Lights? Reflectors?'

The answers to all these animadversions have to be in the affirmative – otherwise, walking or riding, you would never set out on an English road again.

My earliest dream was to cover England, like Cobbett, on a horse. I managed parts of the South Shropshire hills before I realised that far more troublesome than fast traffic on the A 49 was the braying of a diesel locomotive going through Marshbrook station just as I approached the Long Mynd. You simply cannot find enough byways or bridlepaths; sooner or later you hit a main road – or the road hits you. But, for some people, walking, cycling or pony-trekking are as necessary as going to sea – and who counts the hazards of that? Certainly there are no riches to be found on a bike; horses are too expensive to run, and you may not live till journey's end; boots wear out. So where is the gain? Perversely, I think it is in the loss. You lose weight; you lose interest in the world's affairs; you even begin to see England as a magical entity – as Arthur, Shakespeare and Elgar seem to have seen it, sovereign and commanding. You see it as Bede, Bunyan and Blake saw it; and something in your very sinews makes you want to redeem it.

So this book is, as it were, as much about a paradise lost as it is about a paradise regained. Even as we rejoice in the byways and bridleways we shall lament the wide gate and the broad way that lead to destruction. But not so much as to spoil the fun.

Let us begin at Little Ness. I write about Little Ness as TS Eliot wrote about Little Gidding: 'What we call the beginning is often the end... The end is where we start from.'

Little Ness is a 'nose' of high ground overlooking the Severn in Shropshire, next to – but very definitely apart from – Wales. Small but superior, it is a microcosm of rural England, somehow impervious to change. There are the church, the farms, the school, traditionally set in stone. The mound by the church is a reminder that, in the sixth century, Cynddylan the last of the Princes of Pengwern (Shrewsbury) fell in battle and was buried there. Just downstream on the Perry, a tributary of the Severn, is Platt bridge where the light-horsemen 'with a good horse, sword and spear' drove back the Welsh who dared to cross the border line. If they could catch any Welshmen they were put to death, but if the raiders had got back over the border (the river) with stolen cattle they would cry 'Ptroove' (mine own) and the horsemen could not follow. (Gough's History of Myddle)

Industrialization has hardly touched Little Ness. It is an irony of history that one of the descendants of Abraham Darby of Ironbridge, further down the Severn, set up his country estate there in the late nineteenth century, walled off the wilderness which is the Cliffe, and ran it as a kind of rural Utopia. Socially and architecturally, it is still a period piece. Its population has hardly changed over the past two centuries. Bounded by its rivers and hills, it seems sovereign and commanding, in charge of its own destiny. We shall return to it again and again.

A CAUTIONARY NOTE

Written on the hoof as a kind of mobile diary, the text sometimes slips from past to present tense and vice-versa. Rather than tidy this up and perhaps lose some of the freshness, I have left it, much as a panting schoolboy, red-faced, might rush to tell his pals of some misadventure before going to the washroom and straightening his tie in order to report to the beak.

WESSEX

IN 1990, after a lifetime of farming and teaching, I decided it was time to educate and cultivate myself. I could not take on the world, but I had it in mind to try to grasp the nature of my mother country and my mother tongue. It would be an exercise in observation and interpretation. I would deal with it in instalments, a piece at a time. No great plan. I bought a pair of boots and borrowed a bike. Where I could not ride, I would walk. I actually prefer to walk. The bike is something to lean on; from this position you can more easily study the landscape. A comfortable andante is far more expressive than presto agitato, after all.

I would take only minimal luggage: a tuckerbag containing Mars bars and apples which respectively stop one's hunger and thirst, and a back-pack, polythene lined, to hold nightwear and changes of clothes for the day. Trekking is only enjoyable if done on a shoe-string. Ah yes, you need a body-belt with certain resources and information which, you hope, you will rarely be called upon to use. You may, or may not, have a map. Impro-visation is the key. You may have your feet on the ground, but your head is still in the air.

I started in October, that lovely quiet time of the year when things have settled down. I ticked along like a leaf. The Ridgeway led me directly to Avebury. 'History starts here', I wrote in my notebook, propped against one of the stones. I went inside the church, consciously asking a blessing on my quest. I had taken the children there many times. They never could see the little round windows above the north wall, which I regularly pointed out. Children always want to go right up to things. 'Stand back' I would say – they falling over the font and the pews. In those days the bell was on the floor at the west end, waiting to be re-hung. That they could touch and see. Disappointment at not being able to climb inside the rood loft would be followed by disappointment at not being able to play cricket in the grave-yard, so favourably grassed and with a stone already marked for stumps by like-minded children before. They would visit the Keillor Museum to see the skeletal remains of a child from some thirty centuries ago.

I was on my own now, free at once from the embarrassment and the stim-ulus that the company of children provides. One's perspective of history is so solidly blocked by the Normans – particularly by their castles and churches – that it is almost impossible for the mind's eye to reach back even to Saxon times.

One can only privately meditate upon the symbolism of rivers in our religions and their associations with stones. Heaven alone knows what King Alfred, to whom everything pagan was anathema, made of those pagan memorials compared to which the white horse at Uffington was then but a colt. A river of ice had brought these stones here, perhaps ten million years ago. Some three thousand years before Christ, Neolithic man had erected them. But how do you explain to children their 'religious' significance? Or the seismic scale of the culture shocks that, wave on wave, rocked England in the past?

I was on my way now to see something which, I hoped, would be more within my mental – perhaps even physical – grasp. Most people say the Kennet rises above Avebury: 'up Avebury' as the children preferred to say. But I had been to Uffcott before. There is a farm there and two black ponds. There was, I felt sure, some connection between the river and those unfathomable ponds. I hurried to the farm. You can usually get help at a farm. Hardly anywhere else these days can you find a man to ask. I was lucky. I found Bunny Waite. 'I should know' he said, 'I've worked here since 1941!' He told me precisely where to go. 'Up the Salthrop road and on your left you'll see two sheds – old aircraft hangers, Robins we call 'em, they were used for mending Spitfires in the war – there's a path there, it follows a ditch. The Bourne we call it. We moved it once, a bit nearer the hedge, for convenience you see. Then it goes under the road here, through the pond, back under the road below the Bell Inn and under the road again to Winterbourne Bassett...' Bunny knew every inch of these Bourne acres from his rabbiting and birds-nesting days. His directions were clearer than any map's.

There, just as he said, were the Robin sheds – no gleaming Spitfires in them now, but a few straw bales and old implements. There was the path, well a selection of paths, and a fingerpost saying Broad Hinton 1½, Bassett Down 1, and Bincknoll Castle ¾. Yellow hammers darted about; crushed pineapple weed scented my path – it was like a summer's day. The leaves on the trees had hardly turned at all. A two-plank bridge led to what looked like an old pheasant-rearing compound with a low electrified fence to keep out the fox. You could see the hangers at RAF Wroughton, silvery in the distance, and perhaps one house. You are far from the centres of population here. There was a purling in my ear. Was it a skylark? Was it the Bourne?

The path to Bincknoll – Bunny called it Binal – is, like so many Wessex tracks, enchanted. Three-quarters of a mile? I had been walking an hour in my yellow-laced, stout – but cheap – little Czechoslovakian boots. There was a knoll, a slight rise, ahead and a wood; but there was not one path but two, three or four. One went by the edge of the wood, through the young corn; two or three went through the middle between the trees which were no ordinary trees: copper beech, red pine, spindlewood, laburnum and Philadelphus, telling a tale of human habitation hereabouts. But there was no house, certainly no castle – unless it was Merlin's castle. I was in what seemed a small Savernake. Occasionally an opening afforded a glimpse of the flat prairie that spread uninterrupted to the horizon on my right; occasionally the gorge yawned deeper and wider to my left. I veered to the right at a parting of the ways. I had read somewhere about certain lost villages which grew up along the spring-line here.

Here perhaps John Rennie, the architect of the Kennet and Avon Canal, spotted that the two rivers were only about three miles apart and that by forging a link he could make a dual waterway which, like a gold watch-chain, would span the broad belly of John Bull.

It was a watershed, that much was obvious. The ground fell sharply away to the west carrying, no doubt, the feeder streams of the Bristol Avon; and my little Kennet had given me up for lost and gone sulkily, slyly, silently east.

The silence was enormous. I lingered on a mossy knoll, faced with the parting of the ways, still hoping for a glimpse of the castle, Merlin maybe, a new drive opening up, a coach and four, hounds, footmen, portals and Pre-Raphaelite women ascending and descending the steps. Perhaps, I thought, I was Arthur, come to Avalon.

Facing me was a fox, a bird in his mouth – a pigeon I guessed. Close and still. We stood at the parting of the ways in that wood, I and a clean-coated fox. He, brandy-eyed, considered me and I considered him – eye to eye – for one of those endless moments. He was poised, neat and lanky-loined;

young, ardent honey-coated in the sun. He stood his ground, taut, horizontally aligned, his brush aflame. I stood mine – upright, unnatural, a travelling tree: a gallows smelling of human blood, the awkward the unwelcome one. Something of the devil he must have perceived in me, for he slipped away, a bead of mercury, out of sight. Gone back to his coverts, I supposed. But a shared experience had been ours. For one moment we stopped and stared, the sun came out, his eye met mine. It was life on the edge.

Musing, I returned to Uffcott, first hugging the edge of the wood, then following the path of the Bourne. I was lost on a great Gromboolian Plain. A gable point and one small chimney-stack rose out of the rim of corn beyond which might have been ships, for all I knew. Bunny said I'd be late for my lunch. Three sorties of military aircraft rose like silver fortresses in the air, catching and momentarily holding the light. The only other sounds were the distant bleat of sheep, the tinkle of late swallows that must have forgotten to take off, the sucking sound of a magpie and the close munch-munch of a cow. I was back where the river goes under the road. I had seen no water yet, but a damp patch once in the field; but seeing you could hide an aircraft-carrier in this landscape, it is not surprising that a baby river does not show.

TO THE MEMORY

OF

JETHRO TULL

A PIONEER OF BRITISH AGRICULTURE

BORN AT BASILDON 1674

DIED AT PROSPEROUS FARM SHALBOURNE 1740

'Tis in some degree the interest of everyone who lives by bread that true principles be established in agriculture; but none ought to be allowed as such till they have been thoroughly examined. Truth is like gold which the more it is tried the brighter it appears being free from dross.

Horse-Hoing Husbandry 1725

Memorial to Jethro Tull in Shalbourne Church, near Hungerford.

Jethro Tull and Abraham Darby I – late seventeenth century contemporaries – catapulted us into the technological age. It is astonishing to realise how very early they were. Tull's seed drill, my *Oxford Reference Dictionary* points out, made possible the control of weeds by horse-drawn hoe and so reduced the need for farm labourers, freeing them to work in factories. What factories? Well, right here in Berkshire, John Winchcombe had long established woollen mills employing six hundred workers in the Kennet Valley. Thus, the so-called Agricultural and Industrial Revolutions went hand in hand. Nor were the Tull and Darby products – and those of other pioneers – restricted to home markets: they went all over the known world.

Researching Tull is hard work. In his own writings he did not give much about himself away. A biography by G E Fussell, 1973, creates some difficulties while clearing up others. It is particularly confusing about the identity of Tull's mother. Was she named Dorothy? Was she named Mary? The reader ceases to worry. Does it matter anyhow? The important thing for scions of prominent or prosperous English families was that they should marry up. The Darbys proved that.

Our Jethro Tull was, it appears, Jethro Tull III. Mr Norman Hidden, in an article in *The Agricultural History Review* (vol. 37, 1989) has worked it out that a great uncle (Jethro I) who described himself as of Cholsey, Berks, gent, married to Mary Goddard. He was for many years the estate manager for an important family the Husseys, who owned extensive lands in Hampshire, Berkshire and Wiltshire. The family, Mr Hidden says, 'lived above its income....' The point was reached where the profits of the estate were not sufficient to pay the interest on bonds and securities and brokerage of the debts; and the inevitable crash came in or about 1673-4.

Tull, who seems to have owned a sizeable conglomerate estate near Hungerford, made a desperate attempt to save himself and his family by selling off much of the land. He was a broken man – hunted by his creditors on one occasion to distant Wales – '*but*', says Mr Hidden, '*somehow he managed to squeeze out of his losses a farm in the area called (or which by amazing chance was called) Prosperous. He was able to do this by transferring the farm to Jethro Tull II before his creditors could get at it*'. Jethro Tull II was his nephew. This nephew married Dorothy Buckeridge; they were the parents of Jethro Tull III; thus our Jethro was born at Basildon in 1678 but, so to speak, had a foot on land bordering Oxfordshire in the north and land bordering Wiltshire in the south. He was still a wholly Berkshire man.

The family fortunes must have recovered sufficiently to allow young Jethro Tull III to go to Oxford, be a student of Grays Inn, a musician and a young man about town. Town meant London. Tull, it seems, never wished to be a farmer. He studied law, not to become a barrister, but to ease his entry into politics. He had his eye on the continent – whether he actually went on the Grand Tour as a young, unmarried man is open to doubt. Jethro (Hebrew for abundance) himself wrote *'it was accident, not choice, made me a farmer, or rather many unforeseen accidents'*. Clearly the family's financial (and social?) tribulations rumbled on. Jethro chose a girl from the country, one Susannah from Burton Dasset in Warwickshire; married her, not in London as might have been expected, but in her home village; and set his hand, if not to the plough, to the drill. Necessity, as Mr Hidden says, was the mother of Tull's invention. The great wonder is that it was his training as an organist, and his complete knowledge of the workings of the organ, that gave him his best initial idea. As he so clearly records it: *'I examined and compared all the mechanical ideas that ever had entered my imagination, and at last pitched upon a groove, tongue, and spring in the sound-board of an organ. With these a little altered and some parts of two other instruments, I composed my machine'*.

We know from his own account, that when he first came to Prosperous that the farm was *'cut out of the skirts of others'* and a great part of the land was formerly a sheep down. The land was chiefly chalk but with some clay, not well drained and not easily worked. Oaths must have echoed from around the soundboard of his drill!

I first visited Prosperous in July. Here, south of Hungerford and the Kennet valley, the land rises to 150 metres. Tull's old house, much modernised, is called Mount Prosperous. Lady Wills, the owner of the estate, was ill so I only saw the farm manager who, among much else, is in charge of the large Guernsey herd. The bull had recently had an argument with a JCB which had cracked his face down the middle and caused it to stream with blood. He was an Aberdeen Angus, black as a thunder-cloud, and looked as if he would challenge all comers. But he threw smallish calves, which suited the young cows coming into milk. Turned out to summer grass, blonde and buttery in the bright morning sun they vied with the honey-eyed acres of barley that stretched, it seemed, all the way to Salisbury. Nature, as the psalmist has it, decked herself with light as it were with a garment and spread out the heavens like a curtain. I was on top of the world. I was, moreover, convinced that my claim that Tull was one of the greatest of English inventors was not exaggerated. The evidence was all around me. I only wished that Tull could see it too.

One of the first things that strikes one looking in on Tull's life and experiences is the great difficulty he must have had managing his far-flung estates and their affairs. For, in addition to Basildon and Prosperous, he also worked for some time on his father's farm at Howberry, near Wallingford, where he may have first tried out his ideas. Imagine, in an era of poor transport and communication, the sheer inability to be in three places at once! Imagine the poor state of the roads! The dangers to life and limb to a man who suffered all his life from some form of tubercular disease! A diversity of domiciles may, however, have helped in eluding his creditors. The central problem, as he saw it, must have been how to avoid waste; for in those days, it seems, seed was heavily scattered – broadcast – over the ground with little or no attempt to cover it up. Tull, initially, commanded his labourers to do this by hand. They revolted; as they revolted later when he brought out his new-fangled horse-drawn seed drill, which carefully set seed at certain measured intervals in rows at measured distances apart. To them, it must have seemed like a robot! Observation of the laws of nature and their application in a combination of science and economy have been at the heart of advances in farming ever since. To this extent, Tull altered the face of the landscape (for the better, if the present state of Prosperous Farm is anything to go by) and the fortunes of the nation, and his own.

'Come back in September' said the farm manager. 'I shall be less busy then'. It was in September therefore that I set out to walk from Prosperous Farm to Applepie Hill which is not far short of Basildon where Tull was born. By doing this, I would be in some sense paying tribute to the man, treading in his footsteps, and savouring not only the setting of his achievements, but also – in imagination at least – passing through nearly three hundred years of English history.

I was trying to walk as much as possible of the route on public rights of way. There were plenty of them, marked on the Landranger map by dotted lines, wriggly rather than straight, and – like worms – independent, and not given to connecting with each other. Derek, the farm manager, kindly pointed me in the direction of the first, which, according to the map, would lead me through Anvilles Copse, past Anvilles Farm – known to Tull – and Templeton, to Avington Manor and the Kennet and Avon Canal. I was immediately blown off course – seduced into photographing a group of heifers, all looking like Marilyn Monroe – then by a broad swathe of mown grass, one of several clearings in and around the copse which proved to be false trails; then by a rain cloud that blotted out my only compass, the sun; then by the ensuing rainbow which in a landscape of ploughed loam is like a mirage in the desert. I was diverted by hares and free-running pheasant poults. I spoke to a young tractor driver who appeared to have ploughed up the path. 'That's all right', he smiled 'You can join it again up the road'. Hitting the road, I was afraid to get off it. Soon I was at John O' Gaunt School. Poor old John O' Gaunt, he had some trouble with his landlord, King Richard II, some 300 years before Tull.

It interests me greatly, this ebb and flow of land between the great English estates. Nearly all the best land around Shere, in Surrey, I found was parcelled out between just three titled owners. The land ahead of me now, on either side of this stretch of the Kennet and Avon Canal has been, until quite recently, divided between the Craven and Sutton estates. There have always been successive power players in this game of winning land – sometimes literally at cards with enormously high stakes. You can find out very little about these goings-on; but gone on they have for centuries – ever since William of Normandy bestowed manorial rights on his knights. But even a king cannot guarantee an heir; he may, indeed, be conspicuously bad at grounding successors in common agricultural sense.

The churches dotted along the canal tell you something about the substance of past and present landowners hereabouts. Kintbury is full of memorials to the Dundas family; the little Norman church at Avington – my favourite – is part of Lord Howard de Walden's private estate. The lady at the lodge gives you the heavy key – fit to unlock a castle – worn shiny and thin in the middle of the handle by press of pilgrims' hands... The interior is exquisitely chaste and unchanged, with no heavy memorials, no Victorian neo-gothic grotesquery. The church at Hampstead Marshall, where we leave the canal to head up through Marsh Benham on the Sutton side, is up the hill in the wrong direction.

Entertaining me all along the final stretch of the canal – all the way home, in fact – was the shade of the beautiful Lady Craven, Margravine of Anspach and Bayreuth and Princess of the Holy Roman Empire. She was the wife of the sixth Earl. After bearing him six children, she left England for France and travelled in Italy, Austria, Poland, Russia and Greece, surely the grandest of all Grand Tours. She was a musician, poet, playwright and actress. When the Earl died, she married the Margrave of Brandenburg within a month. At her theatre at Brandenburg House, she appeared in such plays as 'The Provoked Wife'. *'My taste for music and poetry and my style of imagination in writing, chastened by experience, were great sources of delight to me...'* she wrote in her memoirs. *'Our expenses were enormous'*.

Gulls played over the freshly ploughed fields of Marsh Benham. The sun was putting on one of its most brilliant late-summer, evening performances. Each furrow was lit on the west side like a long ribbon of black silk. No chalk flints here but pure alluvium. Gulls have always fascinated me. Thrown inland by the autumn gales, how do they find the new-ploughed earth? Line out your field, bring on the plough, cut up the cake, the kittiwake and all his host of brother migrants come. From one first scout sent in, the wind-swept waves arrive, light round the ploughman's head like Carmelites, white-habited, pronouncing blessings on his work; co-habit with the crows, rejoicing in the shares – the upturn in the economy. I like to see them. The farmer needs the guzzling gulls, just as he needs the rooks that flow in with them, but – like oil and water – never mix.

Best, I like to see plovers which, here on the low alluvial land at Marsh Benham, were out in force. The gulls 'sip' the earth, as they 'sip' the surface of the sea, never appearing to land; plovers and curlews have a trick of lighting, like a ballerina, points first, then running along for a few steps, arms raised, then folding them in a beseeching, forward arc. A few swallows, or martins, hawked the stubbled headlands still, their margins narrowed to a minimum. Why do they stay so long, like late party-goers, giddily tempting providence? The gulls already have snow on their coats – and winter in their eyes! I plodded on, like a ploughman, homeward, wearily. Stockcross stretched ahead, above the Bath road, and the woody, uphill Sutton estate, unwelcoming with notices of privacy. I kept to the road, lost in a reverie about gulls, pewits and ballerinas and house martins partying late. A car, coming towards me, stopped. 'I thought it was you when I passed you back there, but I wasn't quite sure'. A lady, my neighbour from Boxford, picked me up. 'Thank you', I said; 'I was a thousand miles away'.

Looking at my Landranger map for the rest of my journey to Applepie Hill, I saw that I would pass by Hangman's Stone, Nodmore Corner, Egypt (perhaps), Heath Barn, Wilkins Barn, Woolvers Barn, Ilsley Barn, before I struck out over Nutfield Down, Shrill Down, Compton Downs and – maybe – Cow Down, as well. It was a fairly eccentric route; although it lay in a generally north-easterly direction, you could not make out a proper line. Such lines as there were on the map were disjointed anyway. I decided to behave in a similarly disjointed, eccentric and abandoned manner.

First I would go out of my way to Chaddleworth, a place that, in all my years, I had never been to. People (such as Charlie our paperman, who lives there) talk of Chaddle with affection. It is old, villagy, remote and gets cut off in winter. If it snows nowhere else, it snows in Chaddle. Parts of

Chaddle are, my map warmly pronounces, 175 metres high. So, before winter sets in, I work out with Charlie how I get to Chaddleworth. 'You can go by the thicket or you can go by Nodmore – it doesn't matter which...' A glance at the OS map showed that it was in the direction of East Ilsley and Applepie Hill. 'Through the thicket to Peasmore' Charlie said; 'I used to run over to see a girlfriend at East Ilsley'. He made it sound like a five-minute sprint. 'You come out by the Oxford road'.

Peasmore church spire is a landmark for miles, erected, a memorial stone at the base says, by Will Coward, Gent, 1737. You would know you were coming to a blessed place anyway, by the inviting little stile which leads you from the main bridleway across a lush meadow which could only be part of an ancient glebe, to a random sheep hurdle and broken-down old wooden gate sprouting string. There the little path runs out to the road past the traditional church farm wall. Discarded tractor tyres, pallets and brushwood hurdles are, you soon discover, the left-overs of racing and farming in a village now aping suburbia. You pass houses called Lark Rise and Las Vegas; the village hall proudly proclaims that this community is recorded in Domesday Book, 1086. There is a roadside pond, but nothing on or in it that I could see.

Tiring of Peasemore, I took the road to Stanmore and East Ilsley. There is no evident footpath. One, I was told, went across a field, recently ploughed up. Another, 'by the pink cottage' went by a barn 'from a stile set in a brick wall'. Seduced by the village hall's blandishments and the sunny duck-pond, I settled for the road, passing the Old Smithy and the Old Post Office, alike inert, on either side. I quickly found a 'Permitted Path, not a public right of way'. 'Persons', the notice said 'may use at own risk'. I am a known risk-taker! A hint of brushwood fencing by the church had set my heart galloping; I hoped to see hoof-prints, but saw only deep tractor tyre impressions, some fresh plough and much wearisome set-aside. What looked in the distance like a white gabled house with a small tower for a chimney might have been a Mormon temple. The 'Permitted Path' simply led me to another road, with no indication of which way to go. A few hundred yards to the left I found a sign-post pointing to Wantage. I doubled back, past my false Permitted Path, and rejoined my former road lower down. I was walking with my shadow ahead of me, so I knew I was going roughly north and east. 'Keep to the left of the sun' I kept telling myself. I had somewhat lost faith in my map.

Rain, unforecast, started to fall. Martins, with as little idea of the distance they still had to travel as I, wantoned over the untidy fields of set-aside. Up sprang a new byway: 'No Dumping' the notice said. (There were plastic shocks of course.) The track was smoothed with wood-chips – a promising sign – and lined with sheltering hawthorn and hazel. Easy to see where the old hurdle- makers cut their hazel boughs. I never saw such quantities of wild fruit: sloes, crab apples, elderberries, clusters of nuts and trusses of haws. There was an embarrassment of choice in the small matter of byways too. There were frequently three signs together, all pointing vaguely ahead. I generally chose the mean – the one that, in some Harry Lauderish way, kept right on. Acorns crackled under my feet. A jay screamed over my head. Some signs were colourfully designated 'Ilsley Downs Riding Route'. Promising. But I found no horse droppings or prints. Other signs said 'Recreational Route'. Maddening! No public sign tells you where the path goes.

Then my path suddenly broke out beside a prairie. A tractor shuttled up and down, ploughing and harrowing in one operation. I noticed that the driver deftly unhooked the harrow at the headland, swung the tractor round, the plough's reversible teeth shining in the sun, hitched the harrow up again – automatically, of course – then set off down the stretched-out field again. I caught him at one of his turns to ascertain the way to East Ilsley. 'Straight' he said – obviously. A hare got up from under my feet, sooty ears pricked; ran a few yards, turned, looked at me sideways, ran again, turned then bolted into a wood. (To add to the North American look of this landscape, the higher ground is blanketed with pines.) The surface of the path was glassy with impacted chalk, perfect for tractors but hazardous – especially in frost after rain – for horses and men on foot. Keeping straight, the path descended to the road. There were tractor tyre marks everywhere – and the reservoirs of water they leave in their wake. The tractor is king. The sheep have gone; the men have gone; the horses have nearly gone.

A new bridleway beckoned. Where, I wondered did this one go? On my right I spotted penned sheep. (Bred up in captivity, perhaps, now being returned to the wild?) A sheep dog set up the usual business-like, I-told-you-so racket while his master (tractor-borne, of course) sorted them out at the far end of the field. I was just pleased to see sheep. This is a fairly de-populated down. Grass ran like a green ribbon down the middle of the lane. I entered old woodland again, soft leaf-litter under foot. There were many and diverse signs: Ilsley Downs Riding Route, Public Bridleway, Public Right of Way, Bridleway, Byway.... The one that went straightest seemed least frequented, but there was a sign of a human hand outstretched, offering food for pheasants in a bin a little elevated from the forest floor.

It is strange how you know, before you see a house – is it by smell or some deep instinct? – that you are nearing human habitation. A stand of nettles, a tangle of barbed wire, are common clues. A deer stood across my path, but, seeing my white face, melted into the wood. The path, going downhill, suggested I was coming to a village or a community. Oak branches had been cut off low to the ground, leaving owl eyes staring out of the bark. So few sheep; abundance of pheasants, but only one lapwing and one skylark.... It is not I that am lost, I say: it is England that has lost its way!

Dispirited, I emerged on another anonymous road. I had no idea of the time, could not see the sun for cloud, it was spitting with rain and I half hoped I was heading south and home again. I picked a piece of late-flowering knapweed, marvelling at its purple glory; then, not totally absorbed, I spotted a bridle-path which, I decided by whatever crooked reasoning, might lead me to East Ilsley. After a short grassy stretch, it led to pine woods and more plough. A hare started up from under my feet, ears pricked, rufous rump raised, back legs extended, tail clamped low. Hares have hind legs so much longer than their front ones that, like some race-horses, their hind legs actually land ahead of the others. By some brilliant stroke of evolution, they are even able to run ahead of themselves! Supernatural, to the point of ungainliness.

Hares, the object of superstition and prejudice in history, fascinate and freeze you by their startlingly fantastic freedom – and solitariness. They were rare to us children at home on our Shropshire farm, having a kind of magic. It is still a great thrill to see one. They have a life unique. They have the clever habit of spreading their young around in separate forms in the long spring grass, to limit the chances of being preyed upon. Then they go off on those long curving runs which make it almost impossible for the swiftest greyhound, trained in coursing, to catch them. My hare, seeing my hobbledy inefficiency, sat sideways, teasingly, then, supple as silk, he left the open stubble for the cover of the trees. 'My hare', I called him; then laughed, knowing that he is free as the wind, and as strong, on these downs. 'So much for land ownership' I shouted to the wide-open prairie. The cloud lifted. The sun came out.

The path, tussocky now, led through the wood to what I thought was another open field. It too was being ploughed. Skeins of seagulls followed as the tractor ranged across and across, the earth turned or turning under my feet. For sure, the sign pointed across the field. I decided to press on. When I reached the unploughed stubble on the far side I waited for the tractor-man to draw close, half wondering if I should demand my path back or apologise for trampling on his finely harrowed earth – for it was quite soft, but not too yielding, under foot. I did neither. He stopped, opened the cab door, smiled and said 'You again!' I said 'Get me out of this mess' or words to that effect. He pointed to a break in the trees which obviously was the start of – or the end of? – another path. 'Straight' he beamed. He seemed to know no rights or lefts. A couple of singing skylarks lightened my step. I found a track which had no bewildering signs like Recreation Route. It led to a deep defile, a friendly beech (which typifies Berkshire for me), horse droppings and hoof prints. My shadow went before me, so that much was right. Confidence entered my step. I glimpsed the dreaded Oxford road (A34), which I truly did not want to see. However, I knew that if I could, by subtlety or bravado, get across it, East Ilsley lay the other side.

I crossed by the friendliest of underpasses, Mr Kipling's Exceedingly Good Cakes travelling on at speed, while I headed for The Swan, a pint and – I still hoped – a piece of apple pie. But, whatever time it was, I knew I was two miles short of Compton and four miles short of Applepie Hill. My precise map told me so.

'Whose lads are you?' I asked the lead jockey of a string of chasers clattering along the village street. (You know a good chaser by its height.) 'Mr Sherwood's' came the reply. I complimented him on their turn-out. There was one, a golden chestnut with white markings, that looked destined for Hollywood and will be famous in my memory if he never wins a race. This was my auspicious introduction to East Ilsley. The village itself is as pretty as a picture and combines beauty with rare character. It has not survived at the crossroads of history without being tough. The name Ilsley is derived from the Saxon 'Hilde-laeg' meaning battlefield. It lies in a fold of the downs, just below the Ridgeway. Its sheep fairs were second in fame and size only to Smithfield. It used to be thick with stables – Summerdown, Montpelier and Nelson House, to name only three. There are thirteen pubs. (Drovers and jockeys are as thirsty as pirates.) The A34 used to run right through it until two ten-ton lorries in one week ran smack into one. Let Mr Kipling's Exceedingly Good Cakes take the by-pass. Here was exceedingly good everything for me.

After refreshment (there is no doubt that pubs make for friendliness in a village) I sauntered by the duck pond, then up the hill to the church. St Mary's is the kind of church I like. It crowns the hill overlooking the town: evidently a site of great antiquity. It is manifestly Norman in origin:

upstanding, but not out of scale with the rest of the village. The interior walls incline outwards. The nave is likewise massive and stout rather than spacious or grand. I crept into the bell-chamber where the bells are rung from the floor and the walls are decorated with official and unofficial memorials of generations of strong-armed Hilde-laeg men and their record-breaking peals. Conspicuous among them were the Hibberts and Chilcotts; and, proving that you don't have to be strong-armed or male, I spotted the name of Miss Marjorie Field.

Going downhill from the church, I fell into conversation with a lady who had been in the Land Army in the war and thus met her husband who worked with the sheep. I said I had not seen many sheep. 'The farmers did so well in the war they took a lot of land which they never should have done and ploughed it up'. Short history of modern agriculture.

On my way to where the sheep fairs were held – marked by a commemoration stone – I spotted a nineteen-thirties plough. I could date it more precisely than the church. I had seen one exactly like it, painted blue and displayed outside the house of one of my cousins in Shropshire. Horse-drawn (in its day) single share, leaning almost rakishly, wish-bone handles raised, it stood on an apron of green outside a white house. These old ploughs are a magnet to me. I only wanted to talk to it, touch it, photograph it, perhaps. 'Can I be of any help' said a tall, handsome man at the door of the house. 'Ohm your plough...' I mumbled 'I only wanted to look at it – perhaps take a photograph... I didn't realise I was on private land'. 'Would you like to come in?' said the gentleman, realising perhaps that I had a sympathetic eye and no malice in my mind. 'I wasn't intending to steal it' I said. 'You couldn't' he smiled 'it's clamped to the ground'.

Indoors, we discussed the plough, but I was taken by the pictures of fine horses on the walls and the pair of riding boots in the hall. Those boots! They shone in the hallway, upright; poised; columnar; classical; dark; polished – verve in stillness, stillness in verve; varnished almost, as a Stradivarius violin; close-fitting; curved; cylindrical; symmetrically matched; of mutual excellence and marvellous elegance; fashioned and finished; honed to perfection in the field; twinned essences of beauty and utility; and – like the violin, so little altered in 300 years – immediately recognised; two pieces of ox-hide, oak tanned; as English as blackjacks; you'd think you could drink from them as many shorts – or 'snorters' – as the Master says you need to fuel you through a long, hard-riding day; they'd hold as many litres, or astride a horse of seventeen hands, as many fluid pounds, and – like the violin – let out no squeak, be none the worse; indeed, be like the bay that darkens with maturity; and, looking at him, 'Royal Stuart', you have no doubt he'll stay!

Suddenly I became aware of, and apologised for, the state of my boots – cheap Czechoslovakian, stubby-toed, smutched with chalk. Standing in the hallway, with its light coloured carpet, I realised from the pictures and the quality of his boots that I was in the presence of a man whose interests extended beyond old ploughs. He told me, *en passant*, that he was Master of the Vine and Craven Hunt. All the time I was looking at Cecil Aldin prints, a superb painting of a ploughboy coolly facing up to a raw colt with dynamite in his eye, and the portrait of the Master's favourite steeple-chaser, Royal Stuart, I was thinking about those boots and trying to hide my own. 'Your boots' I said, on leaving. 'Oh, those are my everyday, plastic ones' he said. 'My really good leather ones are upstairs'. I smiled, but I still kept my poetic picture of those in the hallway in my mind. In my camera, too, I had a really good picture of the 1930s plough. No doubt about that.

There is more to Compton than racehorses, but not much. There is the Agricultural and Food Research Council's Institute of Animal Health, which is hard to get into, and harder still to get anything out of. I hoped to find out what bells the name of Tull rang there, but was disappointed. Plodding on to Applepie Hill, I could find no pub, no pint, no piece of apple pie. From the top I surveyed the open prairie, freshly ploughed as far as the eye could see. There was not an animal or a man in sight. What, I wondered is the future for this part of England: a multi-cultural society in a mono-cultural environment? I began to thank God for the wild roadside hedges which, in their overcoats of Old Man's Beard, at least break up the monotony of the view. I also thanked God for the phone, my wife and her car.

The next morning I motored to Basildon to see what bells the name of Tull rang there. There are two Basildons, Upper and Lower, severed by the busy Wantage road. Everybody seemed to be in a car. Luckily I found a lady who kept her feet on the ground long enough to tell me where the church was. 'It's redundant though' she said. It is down a lane to Basildon Park – so sunk in whatever was its former glory that there seemed, except for cars and Land Rovers, no evidence of life. The church is overblown like Chaddleworth's and points, I'm afraid, to a fate deserved by temples dedicated more to the memory of dead squires than to that of the living Christ. After much poking around, you can just see the pale little memorial stone by the south wall – but you cannot read it. The simple grey granite slab – sadly now looking rather like rendered cement – has weathered badly since its placement there in 1960. With foreknowledge and by a process of sighted Braille – using your finger-tips as eyes – you can deduce that Jethro Tull was both baptised and buried here on such and such dates. That disposes of him.

Mischievously I returned by Aldworth, to see the famous stone giants there. They are effigies of the de la Beche family who ruled there in the thirteenth and fourteenth centuries. Successive monarchs must have valued their allegiance for their size alone: they averaged over seven feet. They lie about the smallish church, taking up most of the room.

'Townsend' taking a well earned rest outside the Richard Jefferies Museum

For my first spins on a mountain bike I chose short runs – the Ridgeway, the Kennet and Avon Canal towpath – then branched further afield. For my mount I borrowed Townsend, one of the early types to appear – an interloper, I think, from Scandinavia. We had certain shared characteristics: off-road instincts, worn sprockets, poor brakes and a tendency to be awkward (and grubby) when the chain came off. Otherwise, we rubbed along fine. If I had been young and fair I could have called myself the Biking Viking. Recollected now, these early rides appear in the present, unrelated to time. They recur like the daffodils that usually accompanied us in the spring, flashing upon the inward eye.

Spring, and I was up and away – rusty and relieved after my winter sleep. A straight Roman road ahead, there was I, one mile out of Boxford, my tent strapped to the seat and crossbar of my mountain bike, my tuckerbag with food on the handlebar; my spare clothes, toilet bag and tools in my rucksack on my back. I developed the theory, educational really, called Beaten by the Hill. I suppose everyone goes through the pain of learning to ride a bike. You get quite good – but you never get any better. I'm no better now than I was as a boy. Nor worse. I was defeated just as badly by the Grange Bank going to school in Shrewsbury as I was by the hill at Sole Woods this morning. You just have to get off. Your knees buckle under you.

Baydon ahead. Swindon 10. There were horsey farms strung out all along this long straight road; reluctant schoolboys with a long, straight school day ahead, turned out early for the bus. I spoke to the lollipop man in Baydon, who, at ten to nine, was just going off duty. He lived, he told me, at the back of the pub. He was seventy-three. He had lost his wife three years ago. He himself was knocked down recently in a multiple crash on this narrow stretch of road. 'I struggle along', he said. 'I had a broken knee-cap'.

Swindon lay flat and featureless below the breath-taking escarpment which culminates in Liddington Hill, the edge of Richard Jefferies' country. I asked directions to Coate of an old man taking something out of the boot of his car. 'Oh, easy' he said. He was German – probably a prisoner of war who married a local girl and stayed. 'You can't miss it.' 'Ow, you want Coate Water', said the maid at The Retreat in Coate. The drive was lined with willows and daffodils – the sort of place I imagine Jefferies would have enjoyed. 'Ow, yow wahn' Cowte Wahter. It's a reverence. Past the Sun Inn'. I wish I had recorded her; she was lovely; pure Wiltshire; pure woolly-bosomy Wiltshire. Coate Water in sight, Sun Inn on my left, I turned into what turned out to be a Country Park. I asked a man by a pick-up outside what looked like an old farmhouse. 'Is this where the old boy lived?'

'No', he said. 'His house is by the Sun Inn'.

I was wondering what he was putting in the back of his pick-up. They were clipboards. Children come here from schools. Pond-dipping.

There is Cotswold stone walling round the three-storey brick and slate farm house by the Sun. There is a large bay window to the left of the blue front door. Jefferies only lived here as a boy. The lawn you can imagine him not wishing to mow. There is a curious thatched annexe with a side door to the same front lawn. Pines stand like brooding sentinels over the stackyard invaded by nettles. The orchard has a gnarled apple tree and gnarled geese. A ridiculous painted milk churn is perched on a stand. Bicycles are dumped in the old farm sheds; a Spitfire (car) stands outside. I walked all round. There was nobody in. On leaving, I paused beside the pig-headed notice. There, on the pavement, I met Butch Cassidy and the Sundance Kid sauntering along. 'Is there ever anyone here?' I asked.

One was stocky, laid-back, leather-jacketed and smooth. The other was tall, lean, over-coated and sweaty-faced.

'Bin to the Railway Museum?'

They had just come out of The Sun. When I pressed them about the Museum here they said, again in unison 'Er's workin' on the motorway'.

'Maintenance?' I asked.

'Now – on the petrol pumps' said one.

'Now – er jus' takes the ready' laughed the Sundance Kid.

If Coate and Swindon neglect Jefferies, Malmesbury neglects Hobbes. Thomas Hobbes that is, who lived only a little earlier than Tull. There is no memorial in Malmesbury to this, the man who was born here, the son of a practically illiterate priest, a choleric drunkard who used to fall asleep in church and 'call his cards in his dreams' and had to be wakened by the Clerk. After Oxford and travel abroad, he obtained the patronage of the Duke of Devonshire. He is remembered for saying that the life of man is solitary, poor, nasty, brutish and short. *'During the time men live without a common power to keep them in awe, they are in that condition which is called war'*, he wrote in Leviathan; *'and such a war is of every man against every man'*. Poignant words from the pen of one who lived through the English Civil War! *'No arts; no letters, no society; and which is worst of all, continual fear and danger of violent death…'*. Hobbes' thought is extraordinarily modern. At the same time, one feels, it would have appealed to King Alfred in its broad philanthropy, encompassing man's every need.

Alfred gave the original Charter to Malmesbury in 880. Athelstan, his favourite grandson and one of the greatest Saxon kings, was buried in Malmesbury Abbey; but the tomb we see there today is, the guide says, a mediaeval fake. What is not a fake, however, is the glorious south porch. Shorn of both ends and its spire, with a great vacuum to the north, where gardens are now laid out, it is difficult to believe that this huge amputated limb once belonged to a body of stone that must have been one of the wonders of mediaeval times – the 13th and 14th centuries when Malmesbury was a centre of the woollen trade and the Abbey rich and powerful. The Dissolution signalled and in 1480 a great storm precipitated its decay. An earlier Saxon abbey had been destroyed by the Danes; another by fire, along with mostly wooden Malmesbury, before the Conquest. The Normans found tabula rasa to work on here. With what beautiful results! No one can describe the detail of that south porch, exquisitely crowded with holy figures – saints, apostles and angels – worked into the cream limestone by perhaps as may hands: a cloud of exuberant witnesses! Open on the lectern was Psalm 111: Lord, how are they increased that trouble me, many are they that rise up against me. I thought of the hills I would have to climb on my long way home.

' *I am nothing religious. All I have is a piece of the universal mind that reflects infinite darkness between points of light'.*

R S Thomas

I used to live and work near Avebury and have always loved the Ridgeway, the Wansdyke and other innumerable and un-named tracks that radiate from this, the earliest centre of civilisation, settled by the Beaker Folk some five thousand years ago.

Now, starting just south of Avebury and dropping down Tan Hill to Alton Barnes, I drank deep of the springs of history. Leaving behind me the Kennet, the river which brought our ancestors questing out of the Thames basin into lands which supplied rushes for shelter, willow for baskets, deer antlers for tools, fish and other animals in plenty for clothing and food, flints for weapons and chalk hills on which to celebrate Mother Earth, build beacons and henges for their festivals of light in spring and barrows to preserve the remains, possessions and memories of their dead. Everywhere in Hampshire flow rivers, similarly easily traced, whose valleys are lush with the green and gold of spring and ripe with recorded and unrecorded history. Here at Alton Barnes were the first signs of Saxon Christendom. Here were, cheek by jowl, two sanctuaries in the fields, which only walkers – and ancient travellers like me – come across; one old and active, the other Victorian and redundant.

My next stop on my way to Winchester was at The Wallops, a pair of villages, Upper and Nether, with its own waterways, characteristic thatched houses, old estates mossed over with memories, leafy glades, foot-bridges, lanes going nowhere, sunk in trees and - like Alton Barnes and Alton Priors – one modern and one ancient church. To get there I had to cross a lot of Hampshire that was old when Alfred was a boy. He would, no doubt, have recognised the long roadside grass, the garlic mustard, cow parsley, dock, Jack-in-the-pulpit, the old wood – especially the yew - the chaffinch, the pigeon gliding over, jigging like a snipe; but not the road. I passed by Palestine, a village so named about the time of the Boer War when our imperialist rulers eyed this level land and thought CAMP, as they did at Bulford, Larkhill, Warminster and Egypt, not far away.

Pearson, the architect of Truro Cathedral, built St Peter's, Over Wallop. It has lovely modern pieces of Elmwood furniture and a carpet, the vicar told me, from the House of Lords. You can see where the stair rods ran across it, leading to the Woolsack.

Nether Wallop church is old. It has leaning columns, old Saxon wall paintings and an old man polishing brasses who told me he does the hedges and lawns as well. 'Go on up by Lainstone through the valley' he said. 'That's where everybody manicures their lawns, have two Volvos in the drive and complain when the village shop closes – but they go to Sainsbury's.' I saw signs to Museum of Army Flying and Danebury Hill Fort. I passed a converted non-conformist chapel, dated MDCCCXLI, stood with its gravestones between the river and the road. I was walking in paradise. There was a thatched cottage, white walled, by the stream, bridge to the door, burglar alarms – a sign of the times – and age-old happy-go-lucky ducks. Aubretia grew on the coping of a wall. A man toiled in his water-logged garden on the other side of the road, away from the river. 'Well, they won't clear out the drains' he complained. 'They' being the Council. Here I saw primroses on a tussocky knoll, real Hampshire hurd-ling, pineapples on gateposts, limes and a house which tells its own story: The Three Gables. Once a single house, it has been converted into two; the first calls itself Two Gables, the second, The Gables.

'You can take the footpath across the field and cut this corner off' said another man digging his garden by the road. It was St George's Day – a festival which, like Good Friday, seems to bring the gardeners out. 'It's marked with a sign, but the landowner has taken it over. It's all wrong.' He went on to tell me how the people used to go on Broughton Down to have their picnics. 'New Age Travellers there now – and filth.' He pointed to three yews just topping the horizon where the road wound round. 'The villagers used to take their picnics there too. It's all changed. There are rare butterflies on Broughton Common. The hippies don't touch the butterflies – but you have to pick your way through the filth.' I could just picture the pinafored ladies picnicking by the yew trees earlier this century. The farmer had indeed blocked off the path, simply by growing a powerful ley, wet after rain, which flourished untrampled now. There were pigs in the next field. NO ENTRY MINIMAL DISEASE HYBRID PIGS. There were more ancient yews. The pigs, recumbent in the afternoon sun, smelt me, turning minimally, lifting an ear, a snout, from safe enclosures behind fences and trees.

At the top of the road, all I could see in any direction was one single farm. I could see what excited W H Hudson about Hampshire in the days when it was over-run with shepherds and sheep. This must be some of the best farming country in the world: undulating, well-watered, never steep, with mixed soils, fairly well-drained, wooded here and there. After the pampas, it must have been heaven.

At the main road to Stockbridge I entered the electric age. An establishment on my left looked like a bleak, abandoned poultry farm. There were pre-fab buildings, a bungalow, overhead girders and lengths of old railway track on the ground. Welding sprang to mind. Well set up, but featureless, Houghton Down Farm showed England as affluent; of that politicians could have no doubt. Affluent and green as politicians are affluent and green, encompassing all shades and persuasions. A dual carriageway led to Stockbridge ahead. Weathered kerbstone, like the plinth of an old grave, was pitted and runed with indecipherable hieroglyphs. Two young Yanks stopped their car and asked me where the Air Museum was. I confidently directed them to the Wallops.

Near the turn to Longstock was a house called Sarum and another with 'Polite Notice' outside saying 'Please Do Not Park in Front Of The House.' The gentry lunching at the Grosvenor Hotel looked quite down-at-heel. An old milestone said 'Winton 8.' This is such an ancient place that I could imagine Earl Godwin, who had lands round here, sleeping at The Grosvenor (or some earlier hostelry) before going on to London and dying of apoplexy in the presence of Edward the Confessor, his host.

It is no wonder legend speaks of Arthur being one day awakened from his sleep and reclaiming his real kingdom; no wonder Alfred fought to keep the Danes out of these prime lands; no wonder William of Normandy eyed Britain; no wonder Edward Thomas, for all his Welsh origins, praised the soft South.

Heat came off the burning dandelions on Stockbridge Down. There were roadside coppices of nut, hawthorn, elder and beech. Tireless chaffinches. The second rabbit of the day ran for cover. This was my third or fourth walk on grass – a treat which doesn't occur often. The road ahead was long, straight, steep. George Herbert used to walk like this from Bemerton to Salisbury for evensong, bouncing along no doubt, on the soft riverside turf, a burst of chaffinch song in his ears. Once, people always walked on the side of the road, on grass, like this. Now the verge is so little used it has sunk into hollows. Travellers trip over tussocks, the splinters of flailed hedges, old bottles, like the wreckage of a battle. Yet there is no one about; the philistines have fled. Walking along, trying to encapsulate the essence of England – what England is – is like trying to list all the indications of spring. It is like catching a chaffinch.

Sun drags from the earth the terrible smell of a dead badger. Men were working in the woods, coppicing. Truly. So the business of hurdle making in Hampshire goes on! We may pine for the old days, but then there was ONLY work – no leisure. Now there's everything: waste and plenty, poverty and plenty; and, as someone told me, nut trees dropping nuts on the ground in autumn which, if picked up, would provide protein for a family all winter.

'Hi', said a girl and boy on bicycles. I sat down to drink coffee by a bank of violets and to comb my hair before entering Winchester and the cathedral. This was Arthur's capital city. I noted the good old Saxon names: Weke Manor and Bere Close; that St Matthew's Parish Church, Saxon, had scaffolding round the stub tower, prams without and a christening within; that the rector was the Rev. Sir John Alleyn, Bart. I was tempted to ask a passing schoolgirl if she knew why Oliver's Battery is so called, but thought she would not.

Pilgrims' Gate is a No Through Road. In a sports shop in the High Street, Slazenger cricket bats, series one, were priced £117. The Wykham Arms, by the College, flew the banner of St George. Next to the head-master's house is the one where Jane Austen lived out her last days. Also nearby, I read: *'Here stood William the Conqueror's Palace, The Winchester Mint, later The City Drapers' Hall.'* There were coaches parked outside the cathedral: Thomas of Barry. Inside, Abertillery Male Voice Choir was rehearsing the Chorus of Hebrew Slaves from Verdi's Nabucco. Five minutes later, it only took a snatch of Mafannwy for me to feel the 'hiraeth', the nostalgia, which is paradoxically an expression of freedom, a sense of coming home.

'The side streets here are excessively maiden-like: the door-steps always fresh from the flannel.'

John Keats: Letter September 22nd 1819

At a quarter to eight next morning, I entered the Cathedral Close. The only sound was the bell calling mostly elderly people, on foot or on bicycle, to early Eucharist. We gathered and entered by a small side door with a notice stoutly denying admittance to 'Visitors'. We were a small, sensibly-dressed, single-minded confraternity. We took up the best positions on small rush-seated chairs near the High Altar. The simple tolling of the single bell put us in a prayerful mood. Old men, perhaps veterans of wars, prayed long on their knees. The old lady beside me moved an envelope marked 'Intercessions' to allow me to sit closer to her. We were a special people. The best silver was set out on a table nearby. The Dean, though he sat in a high stall, was equidistant and no better than we were. Only the officiating priest was splendidly robed. *'Almighty God, unto whom all hearts be open.... '* he intoned in a beautiful voice. He commanded attention by this, and by his great height. He looked as Moses might have looked, praying on Sinai, long arms extended, his blue eyes and pink pate shining with grace.

At a quarter to nine on the Town Hall clock, after supper with the Lord and wine from the Dean, I took the bridge across the Itchen to The Worthys, by a nature reserve, squatting ducks, the Nuns' Walk – the old road to Canterbury. The river is very strong in the town, tumbling under bridges, but breaking into diverse channels in the country; then it seeps along, as if it had no energy at all. In this valley – as unconcerned and undisturbed as the ducks on a Sunday morning – there are sunken willows, old plank bridges and cuckoo haunted reed beds which spread into the fields as they do near Thatcham on the Kennet. I struck up to The Worthys, to people, suburbia and a lady with her shopping trolley in one hand and a garden centre product in the other. Everybody seemed old; but the world was young. At Headbourne Worthy, however, I spotted what looked like a boy walking ahead, springing off his toes like a Red Indian. Three rabbits in the high corner of a field performed their morning rituals. The boy ahead pitched something into the air, amusing himself as boys do. A vintage car, open, with a child in the back seat waving, passed me by St Swithun's Church.

All the way to Itchen Stoke, I reflected on Old King's Worthy School, now a private house, flint-faced, extended at the rear, with cherry blossom all round it. Even before its present aggrandisement, the school house must have been some place to live. The master must have cut quite a figure at the door, stern-faced and looking at his watch, his whiskers bushing out from under his high black hat. I passed a glorious house in park grounds on my left: Georgian, with Paladian features added. Smart Friesian heifers rose from their slumbers and charged the fence to see me. I have always been an object of curiosity to heifers. Worthy Park House, I reflected, must have sold a lot of its green acres to the motorway slicing across its south-eastern approaches, like a smack across its smiling, creamy, Bath stone face.

I came to a typical, modest, Hampshire farmhouse; slate roofed, flint and brick, embraced – as it were – by the characteristic low, thatched wall. It had a pillared porch, painted white, with ivy upholstering the front. Father and son rolled up in a Land Rover, a collie fidgeting in the back; father in an old buff smock and weathered trilby; son in a dark blue boiler-suit. They'd been to look at the sheep. Silently, their paths diverged as they walked away counting, as farmers always count or reckon, in their heads.

A Sunday-shining 1950s Austin Seven passed me, father driving accompanied by mother and child: a real family car. I saw my first bus – the Stage Coach – probably going to Alton. Rooks scrabbled about the inadequate ash and beech, establishing a colony – which would have been simpler in the glory days of Elm Imperialism. Hatch End, Longfield House, Oak Hammer, Shelley Close! Very Surreyish and shrubberied. You could not find a more 'thirties statement. No pubs – but a conspicuous increase of Veterinary Centres in our pet-ridden age.

At Rectory Lane, passing Glebe House, I thought the rectors of old must have been a force round here. There is a lovely view of the river, caught through a haze of bluebells, late mist rising: the veil of the morning. A pigeon clattered up. Peace came dropping slow. I was walking in the sun. Was I walking in the light? That is a lovely collect, the one for the third Sunday after Easter: '*Almighty God, who shewest to them that be in error the light of thy truth..*' Past watercress beds, moss-covered, tiled roadside roofs, a calf in a water meadow calling – a bright, clear, solitary sound – more flint and brick Hampshire homes, a Hereford bull, old tourers – faces shining through open windscreens, heading for Selborne no doubt, and lunch – past swans framed in the arch of a bridge, young beef cattle – Charolais, and some of no particular breeding, reminding me of the country boys at school in Shrewsbury; big-bodied, honest, open-faced, but with a simple look – past a white pony that came to the gate to have its head rubbed – I reached New Alresford. I had an avenue of limes and a path running between which was, presumably, the old road, up and down which, my book says, *Admiral Rodney 'tacked to the pubs which lined this street when he lived here.*'

A shining old Jaguar stalled at the crossroads, enabling me and others to examine and admire it more closely. While I was enjoying half a pint outside the Horse and Groom I noticed how strangely people walked – mostly with difficulty – like me. I studied my book with its meandering 'ifs' and 'buts' about the Pilgrims' Way, no sign of which I had yet seen. Deciding I could lose myself on Tichbourne Down, I set about the task of completing the outstanding ten or more miles of the A31 by ample grass verges brocaded with dandelions. The river kept me company, down on the left.

Steam whistled on the Watercress Line. At Bishop's Sutton, where the old bishops of Winchester had their palace, I read outside the church the Prayer for the Pilgrim: *'O Lord, fill this house with thy spirit. Here may the strong renew their strength…the poor find succour…the tempted power, the sorrowing comfort, the bereaved the truth….'*

There were converted stables across from Gallop House. A Suzuki stood outside a cottage. I stubbed my foot on hoof prints in the hard earth. Two little girls stood with a pony tethered outside a house, all ribboned up for a gymkhana, horse-box to hand.

Ha! Chawton ahead. 'Still scribbling, Jane?'

Such a valley as you never saw lay down on my right. Lowering sun tipped the trees, spilling shade and pools of light on the fields. You can understand why the mendicant friars enjoyed roaming around England in the spring. And John Wesley. And those other old Canterbury pilgrims, skipping along and telling their tales.

Some houses in the Chawton area seem just as Jane Austen described them. In particular, one set back with a sweeping drive, where Mr Bingley might have been seen dead; another, right in the village, named 'Darcy', where HE most certainly would not. I took the underpass to avoid the new road. No stage coaches go through here! 'PRIVATE' said a notice. 'NO PARKING RIGHTS'. I worry about the bombardment of the motor car on our small town defences. There will have to be more road fund licences, hence more and more cars; then tolls to pay for all these new roads.

There appeared to be no accommodation in Alton on a Sunday. Seeing a sign which said 'Farnham 7', I plodded on, under Cobbetty cumulous cloud. A bus roared by empty. The public transport system, I say, is a figment of the Planners' imagination. Roads are what we've got, and roads are what we shall have. It will cost the earth. My thoughts turn for consolation to Cobbett. No wonder he loved these buttery acres. More ROAD IMPROVEMENTS AHEAD.

After many tribulations I reached Farnham at last. It boasts a Castle, Museum, Sports Centre, Theatre, The Maltings. Almshouses overlook the cemetery. I steamed into the Jolly Sailor at 7.30 p.m.

Charles I stayed at Farnham on the night of 16 December 1618. His grand lodging is now the Farnham Library. Another fine Georgian house, the old Grammar School (1872) has become the Adult Education Centre. You cannot help wondering if adults really are better educated now. There is a huge church rearing up into the blue, where William Cobbett lies; also the remains of his wife. You do not think of William as having remains; he is one solid block of imperishable English history. He died at Normandy Farm in the neighbouring parish of Ash.

To leave the town I had to find East Street – which I did by travelling beyond West Street. I studied Wilmer House (the Museum), Stanford House (the Language Centre); both splendid houses known to Cobbett, each with eighteen or twenty windows facing the street; the latter more splendidly bonneted with ribbons of white plasterwork. They reminded me of the women of Middlemarch; there is a certain patient, smiling awareness on the face of fine architecture – solid and enduring, but smiling at grief. I left the town by Garage land. I did not ask the boy giving all those Daimlers and Jaguars (second-hand, G registration: £15,000) a bright and shiny morning face, if they were repossessed. He was confident, no doubt, that the sun would come out, the current temporary recession would end.

East of Farnham the Pilgrims' Way and the North Downs Way begin. Walking was now sheer pleasure. A south wind blew across my bows. The path was quilted with a thousand years of fallen leaves. Someone had had the bright idea of making an allotment here, alongside three heaps of horse manure. The fields by the River Wey, though flat and marshy, are given over to grazing, tree planting, and nothing much in particular. You couldn't see the river, dreamily wallowing and meandering, you just felt its presence. I caught the smell of burning hoof, like incense on the morning air. Round the corner a blacksmith was working on a heavy piebald, so docile he hardly needed to be held by the girl attending him. I gained advice about the road: 'Go straight on up.' A young roe deer faced right up to me on the path, then leapt over all obstacles to the river, pausing to look back, wide-eared, at me. Cherry blossom 'snowed' the woods. This was Moor Park, now a girls' finishing school with basketwork in a window, a garland of dried flowers round the main door; but, my book told me, it was where Jonathan Swift wrote 'The Tale of a Tub' and – because he had known her there many years before as a young girl – the 'Letters to Stella.'

On a grassy knoll by the River Wey, just beyond Moor Park, I sat and ate my lunch in the shade of great beeches. Waverley Abbey, the first Cistercian monastery – Tintern was the second – sat mistily subdued by time some-where downstream. Small ash trees grew, only knee-high to me, where I pondered the wonder of it all: Jonathan Swift, the first Cistercians, the intrepid deer… A great tit sang in a high ash, 'ching-see, ching-see, ching-see, ching.' A little way along the path, a man sprang out from the hollow bole of a beech. He said he was from Aldershot, on a circular walk. He took me by sandy paths to Mother Luddiford's Cave. We studied it: an arch of sandy flint slabs, stacked like slates, overhung with ivy, sandy-bottomed, an improvisation on nature that would have impressed an early railway engineer. Who was Mother Luddiford? Did she bring up children in this place? We returned to the light.

Amid the sweet scent of pines, gorse, bracken, we talked of many things, the leaping, long-legged leprechaun and I: the decline of our society, ancient Waverley, depression... He suffered depression for four years, he told me stutteringly. 'Hey! I know about that' I said. It was no comfort to him. He still stuttered on. He seemed under a compulsion to tell me something. He spoke like an educated – perhaps self-educated – thoughtful man. He was tall, middle-aged, married and unemployed. He had a car that had only done ten thousand miles in four years. He preferred to walk. His grey eyes bulged with the pressure of thought in his head. He talked about Alexander and Daniel's dream. 'It's clear as anything', he said gaining fluency, 'that Alexander's fate is foretold in the Book of Daniel, chapter 8. He isn't actually mentioned', he conceded, 'but there is a goat with one horn and a ram with two... and the goat with one horn overcame the ram with two.' I didn't know what to make of this – my knowledge of Alexander and Daniel being imperfect – and feeling foxed by all this symbolism. Just before I left him, as planned at a fork in the way, he asked 'Can I show you the passage?' He took his bible from his rucksack, unwrapped it from its blue plastic cover, found Daniel chapter 8 with a flick of a practised thumb and we read together: *'Therefore the he goat waxed very great; and when he was strong, the great horn was broken; and from it came up four notable ones toward the four winds of heaven...'* It reminded me of The Book of Revelation – the most unrevealing book in the Bible. There is so much coming forth and overcoming and stamping up and casting down... 'You understand' he asked. 'I understand.' As a young boy, I learned to yes, to be delivered.

Hampshire, Surrey and Kent: the most wooded counties in England, so someone told me. Birches squeaked and creaked over my head. They propped one another up like people in decline. Houses peeped out of clearings, expensively furnished with swimming pools at the rear, tennis courts, great fences and gates, security systems and large notices: 'Beware of the Dogs...' I passed Farnham golf club at Puttenham, prettily situated just south of the Hog's Back, as the guidebook says. 'Fortunately not yet the nine storey high village with poultry farm and vitamin factory of Brave New World.' I wonder! Seale has mown lawns, a golf club, chainsaws, amputated trees and farms with newly cultivated, chocolate coloured earth – the ideal loam: part clay, part sand.

It occurred to me, I had seen no sign for The Pilgrim's Way; only the secular North Downs Way. Cloud came up over Guildford. At Puttenham Common I drank of the best water in England, given me by a sunny blue-eyed old man with glasses, wearing a blue pullover and dancing along, a small milk crate in his hand; the obvious person, I thought, to ask for a drink. He fetched me some water, fresh from his own well.

At Guildford I read in my room about the Royal Free Grammar School, founded by Edward VI, George Abbott, whose statue stands at the top of the High Street, Lewis Carroll's connection with the town, and the cathedral 'to which', my book says, 'travellers will come in a hundred or a thousand years' time, just as we now come from Winchester to Canterbury.

St Martha's, the old pilgrims' trysting place on the hill east of Guildford, was closed. Vandalised. Hackhurst Downs and Shere redeemed all. At Albury post office the postmaster was stuffing his shelves with a new delivery of Beaujolais: an index of the village's prosperity. I investigated the Saxon church, left 'redundant' when one of the Drummonds moved the village, in much the same high-handed way that Cerne Abbas in Dorset was moved. The sight of a happy, healthy peasantry was anathema to some great landowners. A Shetland pony foal ran up to the railings, rolled, raced round the paddock, presented his head to be stroked, ran off, came back, showing off. There is usually among animals or children one that seeks attention more than the rest – almost always pretty, like this. For two hours at Shere I was diverted from my primary path: a diversion it will take me some time to describe.

You know Shere – as you know Selborne, Dunster, Duntisbourne, Weobley, Church Stretton, Chilham or Dunchideock – or think you do. It nestles under the downs, watered by the Tillingbourne; it is a sun trap, a tourist trap, paintable: 'the prettiest village in Surrey.' Sitting outside the pub in the square, I observed the habits of habituées, elderly and confirmed. 'It's a nice place to bring people to', they said. A bonneted lady, back turned to the traffic, sat stout and comfortable on a camp stool, painting the church. A little green man on a lady's Moulton, spun by, raised a hand and bade me 'lovely day'. I had to see the church with its striking brooch spire, slab stone roof and interior, richly memorialised with wood and brass. It is a compendium of church history and architecture: Norman, Tudor, Early English (the heavy west door) and Lutyens had a hand in the lychgate, erected 1902. In the porch is an enlarged photograph, well framed and displayed, of an old lady who looked after the church for many years. She is seen pinafored, heavy keys in hand, opening or shutting the door. It was taken at about the same date that the lynchgate was set there. What a memorial!

I had been given the name of the farmer here; but the lady at the greengrocers told me 'he is hard to catch'. 'Try the farm first; if he's not there, he's at home.' I met a lady at Mill Farm, I believe it was called. Not the normal sort of farm I thought, going in.

'A naughty boy' the lady said darkly – referring to the three year old Jacob ram confined in a pen with only a single lamb penned next to him.

'What do you want?'

'I wish to see Mr Reid'.

'He's at the house, at the other end of the village.' She gave me a pamphlet on The Old Farm. I put it with all my other literature.

'Do you only have two sheep?'

'Two hundred' she said. 'We do everything here.'

Before going into that, I set about finding Mr Reid.

Elm Cottage in Upper Street, Shere is an odd place for a farmer to live. Tiny, sunken, ancient and awkwardly quaint. There is no knocker or bell on the little oak door. (It must be oak to be so durable; as the window frames must be, to have held those tiny leaded lights so perfectly, so long.) The cottage is stone-built, tiled, low, long, strong and stout. It is green and cream – or white, as elder is green and creamy white at this time of year. I knocked with my fist three times. A little man, dressed in green, opened the door.

'Come in.'

I immediately recognised him as the cheerful fellow on the Moulton bike who sped past the pub. The living room was cluttered with papers and books (Iris Murdoch and Dervla Murphy, I observed). Among the easy chairs was one, slung like a hammock, for relaxation it seemed. There was evidence of cooking about the Aga, including bread dough set to rise. One of the first things Tony Reid told me was how he uses blackthorn for fuelling the Aga; it splits so easily, burns cleanly but slowly – and smells so good! How could you not love a man who invites you into his home and, within five minutes, tells you that!

'Cup of tea, and one of my home-made biscuits? We grind our own flour.' The rising dough was advanced as evidence. Conscience and hunger-pangs prompted me to tell Tony I would not detain him. He checked his diary. He rang Clare, the lady at the farm. No, he had no appointment at half past one, no trips, no parties of school children to show round the farm. It is a show farm, you see. Everything was done from scratch: milling, linen and rope-making, spinning and weaving... Tony could shoe horses and went to Orkney especially to learn the authentic way to spin. He did everything himself. And he was seventy. He made me feel a minimalist.

We talked of many things: the decline of society, the importance of sound education, the diversity of soil types in this area. In the presence of this apparently omniscient, practising high priest of agriculture, I kept thinking of Puck, Lob, the spirit of Old England. Kipling would have loved him. He was so full of joy and practicality. I suggested he may have come from the Orkneys.

'No, my father and mother lived and worked here.'

What roots! What wisdom! What joy and serenity! I parted, promising to write. (Tony is dyslexic and finds it hard to compose a letter.)

'Farmer Reid, Shere, will find me' he said.

Settled and sound as his cottage, he will not go with the tide, or tumble in the wind of change.

The Pilgrims' Way follows the chalk escarpment to Box Hill where you encounter the Mole. Sensible people take the bridge across; I delight in stepping stones. Halfway across, one of the stones was dislodged, leaving a great gulf. I took my courage in both feet and leapt across. Joshua's Ladder; a series of steps up the hill. Exhausting. Much gale damage to yews. The place to fly a kite!

Merstham has been quarried to death, largely to create the M25. Tilcon is a big name round here. Godstone, Woldingham, Westerham... The Pilgrims' Way goes on regardless. Only the occasional glimpse of an oast house tells you are in Kent. It is such a pretty county, quartered by road and rail links. Trottiscliffe, Aylesford (where you cross the Medway), Boxley, Detling and Hollingbourne... The path goes down to something like a village. Two advancing matrons cried: 'By the time you get to the Dirty Habit it'll be open! ' A dead shrew was laid out on a flint, nose pointing to eternity. Strings of youth from Sutton Valence School appeared on a paper chase. A female announced she was knackered by the first hill.

At Hollingbourne Manor (Private Residence) I read:

'This stone is for a boundary between the grounds of the Rectory of Hollingbourne and the Inheritance of Sir Thos Culpepper Kt, being an acre extending in a Right line from N to S containing the whole close Bowling Alley, the Green court part of the Parlour Garden with Ye Great Parlour, the Chambers over it, part of the Great Staircase and Sir Thomas Culpepper his study as appears both by ye church terrier and several other ancient Deeds of conveyance... '

Food for thought to keep me going to Canterbury.

The trials of the Medway are nothing to those of the Mole. In any case, as you draw nearer to Canterbury, you find more people prepared to take them on. You do not feel such a solitary fool! Kent, you find, is such a friendly county. It is not stand-offish, like Surrey, for it has nothing but the Channel to be stand-offish about. I kipped at Carena, 260 Ashford Road, Canterbury: a house built about the same time as I was. When its bricks were settling into cement, sometime in the twenties, my bones were hardening on a small Shropshire farm. I perched among those bricks on the fourth storey for two nights. Irene, my hostess, looked like Beryl Reed. She might, I thought, have been on the stage.

'Yoor wonderful!' she told me, after I said I had walked from Winchester. 'Isn't 'ee wonderful' she asked her husband, tightening her grip on my arm.

'What time would you like breakfast?'

On the morning of Saturday, April 30, I killed time before breakfast watching TV and reading the fire drill: 'Hotel guests must assemble at the Front Entrance'. I wondered if pilgrims ever had any fear of fire, cramped and closeted in wooden alehouses and crypts of hospices as they must have been. Smoke must have been dreaded like the plague. My fire was all in my belly – I could eat a horse! Not the starveling 'rake-lean beast' of the Clerk of Oxenford; perhaps one of the monk's. *'Ful many a deyntee hors hadde he in stable,/And when he rood, men myghte his brydel here/Gynglen in a whistlynge wind als cleere/And eek as loude as dooth the chapel belle...'*

Full-bellied, I left Carena at eight, past Cow Lane, past Cymru Am Byth (set in concrete on the pavement), past Papa's Café, over the bridge to the City Wall Walk. Wheels spun on main roads to Margate, Sandwich and Dover. None of these places interested me. King Harry Tower rose ahead. I squeezed by Tudor Tavern, Woolworths, Canterbury Lane.... A taxi door slammed. I caught a bit of the Canterbury accent, more subtle and amusing than Cockney.

At St Thomas' Catholic Church I read, 'This chapel of the English Martyrs has some of the relics of St Thomas of Canterbury'. I had missed the eight o'clock Eucharist, but when I entered the Cathedral there was still an air of quiet earnestness about it, as there is in a milking parlour just after it has been used. Stewards open doors, lift ropes restricting public passage, let in the light. They are free to talk. I hesitated to go into the crypt. 'Go on', said one young man. Another told me about a strange octagonal clock trapped in time on a side wall of the north transept. 'An enigma' he said. 'May be French, may be Dutch – nineteenth century – we put it there because it has a rather loud tick.' I caught the distant sound of choirboys' voices, clear and coolly suspended – almost like vapour trails – over towards the High Altar. My ear is drawn to the elusive, as my eye is to the enigmatic. A spiral staircase twirled into the light. Two boys descended. They departed by a door. Dismissed for missing a beat? No, they returned a few minutes later.

Somewhere in the street outside, flooded now with summer light and tourists, I saw the arms of Corpus Christi College, Cambridge. Canterbury is all medieval and modern: monuments and musak. A microphone boomed: 'Two pairs of jeans for £30.' Birds sang in All Saints Lane. A resident polished his BMW. I found the river and the Tudor houses. A balloon floated downstream. Hardly the river - a side channel perhaps. There were boatyards and a tremendous conglomeration of houses and roofs. Greyfriars, Northgate, High Street were thronged by tourists, clicking cameras and agreeably walking into tourist traps: 'Gaze and be amazed - the more you look, the more you see. ' The sun had gone to their head. I looked, but failed to see anything. Too impatient, I suppose. 'For thirty pounds … two pairs of jeans for thirty pounds.'

At the Canterbury Centre I picked up more literature. There is information everywhere, if only the sieve would hold it. In High Street a second beggar, tall, young and articulate, asked for 'fifteen to twenty pence.' The first, old and crumpled, just nudged my arm.

All the bells were ringing for noon. At the Cathedral, I sat in on the rehearsal of Verdi's Requiem, coming to a close with trumpets blazing, the choir yelling 'Sanctus, sanctus, sanctus', and the fraught conductor, like a demented midget, faced with a monumental jigsaw nudging the next piece into place with his stick. The choir, the local Choral Society, was a tapestry of colour, hanging like washing on a raked staging below the east window, eyes, mouths and throats working in the fabric somewhere, somehow. How did it all hang together? By a miracle, I supposed. As everything is a miracle in Canterbury: the silence, the sound, the sense - and the nonsense - of it all.

'The Cathedral and the mastery of the central tower stood like a demand; but I was afraid, and the fear was just. I thought I should be like the men who lifted the last veil in the ritual of the hidden goddess, and having lifted it found there was nothing beyond, and that all the scheme was a cheat... I found nothing but stones.'

Hilaire Belloc The Old Road

It is true that the Martyrdom, the supposed spot where Thomas was murdered, is a void, artfully overhung with what looked like a pair of old scythe blades painted black. I was more impressed to read on a plaque that Archbishop Runcie and Pope John Paul knelt there together in prayer in 1982. Christianity is about a living Christ. Perhaps, I thought, that is what is wrong with England. It is too burdened by its glorious and inglorious past. It needs to free itself from the incubus of history and step out into the present - as we pilgrims did that afternoon in Canterbury, *en fete*, in the sun.

The world comes to Canterbury: Japanese, Germans, Scandinavians, New Zealanders... It is vibrant with amplified skiffle and pop. *Libera me*! For this, not Thomas, had I consumed a hundred apples and Mars Bars and built up my body with oranges, cod-liver oil, garlic, high-fibre cereals, fish and feverfew!

The boy in McDonald's corrected me when I asked for chips: 'fries' he said, but topped up my flask with water and added ice. He, like everybody, smiled. I took no notice of the auburn-haired girl in a medieval green gown who stood all day by the Cathedral gate, handing out leaflets for a performance of the Canterbury Tales; nor much of the Morris Men; nor of the kilted Scotsman piping 'Scotland the Brave' in the Buttermarket. I headed for Woolworths and more sugar to keep up my energy for Evensong and the unpredictable train journey home. I cut across the town to see St Augustine's Abbey grounds - startlingly bright with ephemeral daisies and dandelions - and the old St Martin's Church. This ancient shrine, set about with yew not people, is on just the same scale as our old church at Little Ness, Shropshire; distant on a hill, dedicated to the same saint - funny old Martin of Tours, who gave only half his cloak to a beggar, and what use was that? My path was crossed, as I left by the lynchgate, by a friendly black Canterbury cat.

My feet, till now aching and protesting, were suddenly refreshed. I study the art of walking all the time, changing my socks and varying my pace *en route*. Walking, if you think about it, is the skill, next to talking, earliest acquired and most prized by infants and their proud parents, but often the most neglected in later years. Universities should add to their Schools of Languages, Mathematics, Natural Sciences, Medicine and so on, a School of Walking: Gradus ad Parnassum.

Sitting in the pedestrian precinct of the High Street, the Buttermarket and the Cathedral Close, I reflected on many things - not least how Augustine came to Canterbury. He must have come partly on foot, after landing in Kent to re-found the Church of England. He met with opposition, my book says, from the Celts, or their representatives, still surviving in Britain, at variance with Rome on questions of discipline and practice. Those disruptive, disturbing, druidic Celts! But at the pealing of the Angelus, though not quite the ending of this auspicious day, it was time for Evensong. At this hour the Cathedral was still bustling with tourists, quick to flash cameras and remarks. Only a drab dribble made its way to the chancel to sit with the choir and subdue all worldly thoughts. Indeed, it is for us battered pilgrims, a chance to drop our rucksacks and free ourselves completely from care. We only needed to show what we were made of in the hymn at the end. For the rest, the choir - splendid in surplices and cassocks, intelligent faces shining out of stalls, illumined by candles and elbow-grease - did all the work.

In the first Lesson, we heard God telling Moses how he should set up the tabernacle and cover the Ark of the Testimony with a veil (Exodus, 40): in the second, how Christ was tempted in the wilderness. I reflected on the many 'pinnacles' I had foolishly aspired to in my life; the stones against which I had dashed my foot; yet how marvellous God and his angels had borne me up. The canticles were by Orlando Gibbons and the anthem by William Byrd. For these, the sub-organist accompanied the choir, standing, as the great sixteenth century composers themselves would have done, at a small portative organ set near the choir. I noticed that the singers, like Kent people generally, do not sound their consonants. The psalms were the last great four, so it hardly mattered - they are so well known - and the anthem was in Latin, 'Laudibus in Sanctis.' Byrd, perhaps, would not have approved of all this smoothing and polishing; but my ears relished the polyphony, my eyes looked to the present; and it was the nearest I shall get to heaven while I am on this earth.

I had, however, a trump card up my sleeve. The Dean, alone of all the churchmen I wrote to before my pilgrimage, had consented to look for me after the service ended. He and I had made careful arrangements with the steward to make sure that a meeting took place. I had informed the Dean by letter that I would wear a yellow rucksack. At the close of the service my feet almost failed me. I, who had centred my thoughts too much on my physical self 'til now, suddenly saw myself as nothing, a tiny wordling in a holy universe, a speck of dust on the floor of the firmament of heaven. Everyone I had met had been unfailingly kind, and the steward was no exception. He accompanied me to the side of the chancel where the Dean was talking to a lady in yellow. After a moment, he smiled handsomely at me, remarked that he had spotted my distinguishing rucksack and handed me a small printed card: 'Proof that you've done it', he said. It bore his signature, under the blue banner of Canterbury, the white cross, and the letters IX.

There is too much to ponder in those two letters - symbols, I think, of the early Christian church; but the words that I took away from Canterbury were those whispered over my bowed head in the Eucharist by the Dean at Winchester: *'Preserve thy body and soul to everlasting life.'*

A dark, defensive hill sweeps to an endless, sunlit plain. You come to Edington in Wiltshire full of hope and certitude. You have pedalled easily along the level tow path of the Kennet and Avon Canal. You have seen the greensand fields of what Cobbett described as 'certainly the most delightful farming in the world.' King Alfred's statue in Pewsey may have shrunk, but the little Saxon church at Alton Barnes (Awel-tun: village by the streams) is a continuing blessing, smiling through its flint walls; it sets racing what little Saxon pulse you have left. Agustus Hare ministered here in the nineteenth century 'beloved of his flock ' to whom he dispensed boots and clothing from his rectory: one of the first Christian co-operatives.

Great and Little Cheverell remind you that you are still in MOD country, heavily defended. You pass a prison at Erlestoke. The road is a low defile along the lip of the hill with a series of villages: Coulston, Tinhead, Edington, Bratton, somehow lodged there before going on to Westbury and Frome. You can easily miss Edington. The village itself falls away and peters out into fields. The Priory is a place apart. Other people live in Edington, subtly secreted into side streets; but this is the House of God. It stands there facing you and the hill, with its back to the Plain. It would not fall in a thousand years. Ein ' Feste Burg. It stands like a rock, out-facing the rock which is the hill from which Alfred beat back the Danes, staining the roads with their blood, and forcing Guthrum to sue for peace and be baptized. From the trim lawns of the Priory you fancy you can see Chippenham again, Bradford-on-Avon, Bristol perhaps, where all the rivers of this part of Wessex wind out to sea.

What certainties this great grey edifice inspires! You told the children about it when you first saw it all those years before; how a convent was first founded here, details of which are in Domesday Book; how William of Edington became Bishop of Winchester (1345-1366) treasurer and chancellor to Edward II and First Prelate of the Order of the Garter; how Wm Ayscough, Bishop of Salisbury, was dragged from the high altar by the mob and murdered on Golden Ham above the village - part of Jack Cade's rebellion, 1450; and, of course, how Alfred surprised the Danes. There are no half measures here.

Edington grows on you. There are no cloisters. Plain at the back, there is nowhere but a plain recess or old doorway where a plain lady in a plastic mac may sit on a stone step and read her Barbara Pym. The first spots of a thunder storm, that always seems to be prowling around the hill, drive you inside where the spirits lift. It is not just the fan-vaulting and Gothic majesty of the nave, nor the spidery Gothic in the chancel, nor the clerestory, nor the memorials, nor even the great stained glass, it is the greatest gift to man, after the King James Bible and Cranmer's Prayer Book, the music of the Church of England.

There is one week in late August each year when Edington is host to a Festival of Music within the Liturgy. It is as if all the Camberwell Beauties, Swallowtails and Chalkhill Blue butterflies decided to emerge and congregate here at once. And the angels to join them. At any time of the day when you enter the church there is music in preparation, practice or performance. The organist is running through the chants or trying out the registration for the voluntary; the director of the Festival, who is a good tenor, sings one of those essentially English songs by Finzi or Dowland or Purcell. A rag-tag-and-bobtail of choirboys dribble in to be rehearsed in introits, invitatories, canticles and psalms. And there is no charge for all this gold. It leaves you feeling that God is the fount of all goodness, the Father of all mercies, and that we, his unworthy servants, should give the Church of England most humble and hearty thanks. You would not want to give up the South Porch of Malmesbury or the West Front of Wells (also free) but you would count them as nothing compared to this music.

Solemn Evensong does not start until 8 p.m. but you hang about Edington for however many hours it takes, popping back into the church to hear another glorious cloudburst of praise, poking around the web of streets with their clusters of houses, caught like flies all huddling out of sight of the big, dark spider, the Priory Church of St Mary, St Katherine and All Saints. You find a Craft Fair, conveniently sited opposite the pub. Let it thunder and lighten and rain like hell! In a wide open space of blue sky, you suddenly see how high the hill is, how battle-scarred by man's or nature's ravages; battalions of clouds rove overhead. The battle is re-enacted in your head. Alfred, the old harper, rehearses the ballad-epic insistently in your ear. It must have been here; it must have been so.

At half-past seven in the evening Thor has moved over to Chippenham, blackening the Plain. Here it is all freshness and light. The air is somehow gilded with expectation. The lights are on in the Priory; past cottage gardens still thronged with bees, a throng of people come. It funnels through the Green; it stands outside the door, wide open now. There is still some practising going on inside - some detail being tidied up. Where do all these people come from? The ladies all look as if they ride side-saddle to hounds; the gentlemen, by their military bearing, have retired, like Thor, from Salisbury Plain. They are all rather elderly. A walrus of a man sees you to a pew. It is run like an army exercise. There is no slackness here. No changing your mind about the seat. But the sound is the thing: you know you will hear every well-drilled syllable; and that it will be even sweeter by the time it reaches you at the back.

The practising stops. The choirmaster is satisfied. What time for them repairs, for us eternity will mend. Extra chairs are brought into the nave. Still the proud, but rather drab, people of Wiltshire come: the women in hand-knitted cardigans and tweed skirts and sensible shoes; the men in raked-out suits or anoraks, like me. Only one rather pretty white-haired lady has any curls; the others seem to have done their manes with a curry comb. And the men. There is quite a hum. Tightly squeezed together, five or six in a short pew with a man on a chair at the end, you crane your nose away and your eye towards the west door where the choir - now fully robed - enters accompanied by priests and candle-bearing altar boys. One is swinging a censor. The priests are gilded and brocaded in their copes. The air thickens like soup. You feel you might bolt like an ill-bred non-conformist colt. But you are held in the starting stalls. The race to heaven is underway.

The organist strikes a ceremonial chord. Dumb-founded almost for the rest of the service, you sit while cantoris and decani chant *'O let mine ears consider well... Who may abi - ide it?'* transfigured in a web of high polyphony. You have to leave before the end, tip-toeing out with sundry 'Excuse mes' as vault on vaulting voice leaps over the spellbound effigies, alive and dead. Alike, in corners by the doors and even slumped around the yew tree in the churchyard and on the well-lit green beyond, are young men and girls intoxicated by the sound. 'Where do they all come from' you ask a man standing, apparently sober and awake, by the church wall. 'They come from all over ' he says, as if that explained everything about this seven-day wonder of the world. You come down to earth, pedalling home in the dark on a bicycle. You meet no one now, or in the days and weeks ahead, who knows about it. You read about it. You tell people about it. It is like all mysteries, miracles and revelations; private and impossible to explain.

Spring, and I had recovered my equanimity. I had a new game on my hands. It might even be a winner. It is called 'Spot the Guard's Van'. Having established at Newbury railway station that my bike and I were on the right platform for the 10.21 to Exeter, I asked anxiously of an official which end the guard's van would be. 'This end' he replied. The train - on time - rolled in. A long train. A very long train. I was at the wrong end of it, if end there were. I raced from the unattended rear to the front, the length of the platform, crowded with people all jostling to get on, or off. The guard's van door was open. I was instructed to install the bike properly. I fought my way back to a passenger carriage - any carriage, whatever class. Gone are the days when porters and station masters paraded for the benefit of their customers. Trains don 't stop at stations like Newbury for more than two minutes anyway.

Relieved, I settled down to enjoy the journey through Pewsey, Westbury and Taunton. It is like leafing through a favourite picture book with white horses; farms set among apple bowers; buttercup meadows; red splashes of arable land on hills; the sudden glare of oilseed rape; weirs shot with silver; clusters of cows, horses, sheep - not genetically modified but bearing the variegated colours and conformation of earlier, happier days. Then there are the Somerset Levels - unbelievably flat and low-lying, resistant to drain, Dane and plough. You wonder how any road could be made across this sponge of evergreen earth through which nature has threaded only circuitous, sluggish canals. Our train, however, zoomed along like a hovercraft. One's eyes were drawn to the red tower of Taunton church, pointing to heaven - and the moral that co-operation with nature is better than strife - as any fenman or Hollander knows. Certainly Taunton's tower is testimony to the wealth brought to this region by sandstone and wool.

Hidden in the text of this straightforward narrative are the jewelled names of places like South Petherton, Seavington St Michael and, my destination, Ottery St Mary. They are marginalised now by roads which, like the railway, hurry on to Penzance; but I remember days when, swapping between the A30 and the A303, I could embrace Zeals, Penselwood, Ilminster and Ilchester and still get to Exeter for evensong in my MG. I was haunted by a jumble of Anglo-Saxon, Brythonic and Roman names which beautify this countryside: compound jewels like Compton Pauncefoot, Shepton Beauchamp, Huish Episcopi, Kingsbury Episcopi, Evercreech, St Michael's this, St Michael's that - and all those Clysts! (Clyst means stream and Creech means hill: it is easy to see how treasured is the least height above sea level here.) With this in mind, I came to St David's, Exeter.

Whom God would destroy, he first sends to Exeter. Like some reincarnated Roman, I sniffed the wine-like air of Isca Dumnoniorum whose enchantment no amount of traffic pollution can destroy. Besides, I had found my bike. We climbed St David 's Hill. Many a Roman soldier must have marched up there from the river to Northgate. I, with the benefit of hindsight, marvelled at Russell and Brown's 1834 iron bridge. Pizzerias have sprung up, which perhaps a Roman would have welcomed. I passed them by, heading for the Gothic cathedral whose west front smiles a welcome. It is the widest, warmest smile in the world. A thousand other people have succumbed to its Mother-earth charm. They - we - lie about like Lotuseaters on the greensward in the close. People from all over the world. Seduced by the warm, wine-like air of the west. You would not be surprised to see Drake or Raleigh step out of Moll's Coffee House, the Bishop step down from his white marble seat, or a Roman centurion come up from the Quay. (In today's terms, however, they would all seem over-dressed.)

I was - as always - half inclined to stay, no longer roam, permanently popping into the cathedral and the refectory for spiritual and physical refreshment. Here it seems always afternoon. Evensong claimed me, caressing me with Wesley's anthem 'Blessed be the God and Father of us all'. I then rode out to Ottery.

It is easily said: rode out to Ottery. It was only eleven miles. It was a fine spring evening. Blossom scented the air. I believed the wind was in the west. It would blow me there. My sister lives in Ottery. All winter I had been reading Richard Holmes two-volume biography of Coleridge, who was born there. It, like Exeter, had worked its enchantment on me. I could not help myself. 'Which is the best way to Ottery St Mary? ' I asked several folk, giving it its full name for clarity 's sake. I got no clear answer back.

'Mmmm.....'

'Funny you should ask that' said a lad leaning on a bollard by the Broadclyst turn, 'I'm just waiting for a lift to take me there. This road goes straight there.'

Who was I to argue? My map suggested Clyst Honiton might be better. One Clyst was much the same as another, it seemed. Evening sun threw my shadow ahead of me all the way through Pinhoe, Dog's Lane and Whimple to the A30 and Fairmile, where I began the long descent to Ottery via the old Honiton road. Many times in the past I had been tempted to stop at the Country Restaurant for cream teas. Tonight it was closed.

Past King's School, the hospital and Cutler-Hammer (old mill) I span till, disorientated, I entered Mill Street from an unfamiliar angle, dismounted and walked. I was several houses past my sister's, in a dream of Coleridge and spires, when she called from her terraced house and hauled me in. I told her about the maze of lanes I had been in, festooned in cow parsley, mignonette, spurge and apple blossom; about Orchard Cottage which I photographed, derelict but romantic with its old Devon sandstone rouged by the setting sun, bearing up under the weight of centuries of bearing fruit, like an old lady in her bridal gown. I told her about stopping to ask a man chopping wood outside his cottage (you know how that musical sound of the axe draws you in), about the varieties of apple that are grown so abundantly hereabouts.

'Yarlett Mills, Newton Wonders and Brown Snouts' he said. Thus I unburdened my lore which no one but I could understand.

'Tomorrow we will walk to Sidmouth along the river, as Coleridge used to do' I announced, only half remembering what I read in Richard Holmes' biography about a sandstone cave under an oak tree in a field... the Pixies' Parlour where Coleridge scratched his name... a damsel with a dulcimer..., and caverns measureless to man...

It turned out that Devon's riverside paths are even more sinuous than its lanes; it turned out that my ideas about the course of the Otter are as insecure as Coleridge's dream of Kubla Khan. Though twice five miles of fertile ground we trod, we were hard put to it to see a sunless sea; and, though we picnicked by a weir, we saw no sandstone cave resembling a Pixies' Parlour, no Abyssinian maid.... We ran smack into a herd of Charolais bullocks knee-deep in mud and, because the path was wired off, headed with relief for the road. After Tipton St John, Harpford seemed but a hamlet. It turned out to be a rambling estate with House, woods and a Common on either side of the river. This was indeed the Ottery Valley, though it descends not to Sidmouth but to Buddleigh Salterton. We struck east along the main Lyme Regis road. It was like walking on the edge of an uphill tunnel, fast trucks hurtling mercilessly both ways. At last we came to Bowd - a mere four miles from Ottery. It was a long trek still to Sidmouth, but downhill and with less chance of losing an arm or a leg. Time for a cup of tea, a quick look at the sea, and we were glad to catch the last bus for the six mile journey home.

Next morning, I reacquainted myself with Ottery; the tiny town on the hill with its Paternoster Row, Grandisson Court, ancient school, Chanter's House and College, all set about St Mary's Church. On the wall of the church, I ran my finger over the lead engraving of the words *'He prayeth best who loveth best...'* written under the grey, embossed head of Samuel Taylor Coleridge. It is hard to think of Coleridge as anything but young. He is like clear spring water, like apple blossom, to my mind. It is wonderful to think that, as a child of the parsonage here, his simple words - so simply etched on this memorial - may mean more to the traveller than all the sermons his father or anyone else ever preached in this great Gothic church.

Where to go next, was the question probing my mind this beautiful spring. Where but to the silvery Cornish coast and its ultimate point: Land's End. There was no time to think twice. You do not sit counting the miles, or the cost, or the 'presentable' clothes you have with you. What really counts is a camera, memory being worse now than when you were at school. And fruit (apples and oranges) and water in a light-weight flask. Ultimately - especially at Land's End - drinking water is the most precious thing on earth. Water, this year was everywhere, especially in the West Country. Sheep stood up to their hocks in fields awash with it. You silently blessed them as you passed: 'Little lamb, God bless thee.' In Cornwall, however, as I staggered up the (surprisingly) high coastal hills, the sheep stood up proudly on greener slopes: solid Suffolks mostly, with perhaps hardier genes. One hoped so, anyway.

Towns, Guest Houses, Tourist Information Centres, believe me, pale into insignificance to sheep. I have always thought them to be the best indicator of the health of the countryside. You see churches all the way from my present home town, Newbury, to Sherborne, Ilminster, Taunton, Tiverton, Barnstaple (note that name!) to Penzance which remind you of the wealth accruing from sheep. That was why the foot and mouth plague was such a jolt to our national well-being.

Clovelly was probably the last place where I actually passed through a disinfectant point. I longed for a farm B & B and a chance to hear how things were. There, at Higher Clove Top Farm, they had no vacancies. I rode on to the Heritage Park, and rode out again. I was not going to be humbugged with Heritage. I found an old lady who welcomed me in but begged me not to smoke in my room 'cos o' the thatch', and even asked me to get up early 'cos I have to go to have my eyes tested in the mornin'.' I was in heaven. I walked down to the village in the evening, as advised, by Wrinkleberry Lane, kept open for the children to go to school. 'Make sure you go right down to the harbour' said my landlady: 'no cheatin' now!'

No cheating from there on. Land's End did not make any concessions. Three pounds to park a car - but not my mountain bike. Blown there by an easterly, I was blown away by a westerly to Penzance, and the Mayor's Concert in which a prize-winning schoolboy from Sennen spoke splendidly about his old Fordson tractor, part-owned by his grandfather. Lucky lad!

It is remarkable how, in coastal Cornwall in the south, fishing and the sea take over from farming and the land. Tourism adds to the detachment.

Cameras click at boats, not sheep. Mine clicked at Truro Cathedral, one of my favourites and the first I ever saw: ochreous yellow with green copper spire, perfect in spring. Perfect too were the cliff-top views at Porthcurno, Minack and Lamorna; not to mention the Penlee Gallery Exhibition of S J 'Lamorna' Birch's paintings at Penzance.

I had set out with sketchpad and pencils (unused till Penzance) but the sight of South Cornwall's colour, creamy and subtropical, caught so magically, was like a blow to the solar plexus. It also wiped away the grey memory of Land's End and the sea perpetually pounding the cliffs - officially declared unsafe. Even Lamorna Birch drew back from painting Cornwall's wild flowers - apart from impressionistic splodges of gorse. I had examined periwinkle, primroses, daffodils, violets, Neopolitan or 'three-cornered' garlic (like the summer snowflake), minute saxifrages, spurges and infinitesimal ferns all the way. With Blake, I had seen a World in a grain of sand/and a Heaven in a wild flower.

After a quiet sleep and a sweet dream at Ottery, the railroad home.

'Are you sure the 12.04 stops at Newbury?' asked my sister.

'It never has in the past - we might find ourselves going on to Reading or London.'

Uncertain as ever about my destiny, I assured her that it did. I had tickets for myself and my bike to prove it. I rode on from Ottery, through Cadhay, Rockbeare and Clyst Honiton - the route that I might have taken before. I used the A30 because it was there - and it got me to the Cathedral in time for me to rehearse my rudiments of rib-vaulting, pointed arches, piers, bosses, and all the elements of the intoxicating Early English style. At the far end of the Close I found the medieval Bishop's House with its ornately carved porch and inner white walls overhung with wisteria. It is pure England; timeless yet fragile; the work of man in co-operation with nature; harmonious, melodious and subtle as Coleridge's verse.

'Are you sure the 12.04 stops at Newbury?' asked my sister - who met me at St David's, having taken the bus.

'Of course', said I with added certitude. I was more concerned with where the guard's van would be. The train rolled in. A long train. A very long train. It might be positioned at the wrong end. A girl in green, near the rear, stood with what looked like a ping-pong bat in her hand. The guard's van was open. She was the guard!

With the bike properly installed in the guard's van, we were settled in our third class seats when a faint announcement came over the tannoy, of which

I catch only the words 'passengers for Westbury, Pewsey and Newbury'. The voice tailed off.

'Perhaps we have to change at Taunton - or Castle Cary....' A cloud passed over my sister's already troubled brow.

'Perhaps', I said. 'We'll see.' It may have been a Great Western train, but it showed no sign of hurrying.

'We get to Newbury at ten to two' I confidently predicted.

'Jean's meeting us with the car.' Jean, my wife, is never late.

Taunton's church tower still pointed to heaven. There was no announcement that we needed to get off. We resumed leafing through the favourite picture book with its white horses, farms set among apple orchards, buttercup meadows and red splashes of plough-land on Devon's humpty-dumpty hills. Then we sank back into Somerset as into a water bed. There were the circuitous, sluggish canals; the petering out, improvised tracks leading only to an opening into a field. We took in Castle Cary and all its small town wonders at a glance. At Westbury and Pewsey the train drew up, just as one had done at Adlestrop. The Kennet river and canal slipped by, courting each other, hand in hand.

'We have walked along the tow-path there' I said.

'I remember,' my sister smiled.

The train deposited us at Newbury. My sister's luggage took up most of the boot of the car.

'I'll ride' I volunteered. 'I'll be home before you!'

But this bit of bluff I did not believe.

MERCIA

Spring in The Bowl of Plenty

IN this section I include parts of Wales which, if only because of the twin sources of the Severn and the Wye, cannot be ignored. The Bowl of Plenty extends, of course, to East Anglia; but that, to an adopted southerner, can be more easily embraced en route to the north. Here we explore Kilvert's association with the Wye Valley and the influence of the Darby ironmasters who became landowners, particularly in Little Ness in the valley of the Severn.

> *The source of the Wye, which is a little pool, not much larger than that which constitutes the fountain of the Severn, stands near the top of a grassy hill which forms part of the Great Plynlimmon.*
>
> George Borrow Wild Wales 1862

Note: Plynlimmon is variously spelt. Pumlumon seems more correct.

On my 23-gear mountain bike, Townsend, head down through the Vale of Gloucester and the Forest of Dean, Hereford and the Wye Valley were well within my range. I fancied Hay and Clyro and Bredwardine: Kilvert land. Two miles out of Hereford, however, you still can't see a sign for Hay. A schoolboy waiting for a bus, shining morning face and shining tie, did not know. 'Rhayader 43...' People all go to work, leaving their dogs in charge.

There is no one to ask. It is a wonderful road, however, mostly downhill. Beautiful hills and fields full of lambs. A smart white manor house, set about with cedars, pines, oaks in parkland. Very, very Herefordshire.

Ah, another house - now a Nursing Home, the notice said. National Trust Exhibition. The Weir Gardens. Down by the Wye. I wandered over two cattlegrids. 'Dogs restricted to car park' it said. At a gate I met Dick.

'We're not open till eleven' he said; 'but Tom and me are retiring today.'

'My first name is Tom' I said.

'Mine's Dick' he said.

'Where's Harry?'

'He's comin' to take over.' He laughed and he let me in.

This, I thought, is what I came to see. A bend in the Wye, draped with willows, the bank studded with primroses, daffodils; the sloping gardens beautifully tended; walkways; terraces; rustic arches; palings; a boat-house; the shivering surface of the river like a snakeskin … seats set about… But I could not sit, being a restless, intoxicated dreamer. Tom and Dick were burning dead leaves - winter's dross - and other odd blemishes to the scene, setting up a series of blue smoke plumes which lazily climbed the tree-lined hill beyond. How many times had they done this, I wondered; quietly allowing nature complete freedom to restore herself each year. You could hardly imagine such gentle men cutting anything down. 'We're just tidying up' they said.

Yews and cypresses smelled of turps. A massive hornbeam was festooned with catkins like soft cornflakes. Beeches, newly leafing out, crowned the hill and fingered the slope with their roots. Speedwell underlit the daffodils with its porcelain blue light.

'A C Parr, big whisky people from Cheshire, owned it' said Tom. 'Taxation killed it, yo' know'. (How often have I heard that!) I wished them luck - and Harry, taking over. 'We'll be back' they said. 'But it wont be so tidy!'

I passed other huge estates that day. Stuccoed houses, magpie farms and churches punctuated the periwinkled, cherry-blossomed route. I saw only two Hereford heifers in a field, but they were beauties too. Quality, not quantity, is required now. Still no sign to Hay. I tried to enquire at a house with the gate open and a car in the drive. There was a pair of child's trainers upturned on the front step, a pair of spectacles on the windowsill round the side. There was no one about. Gardens are not worked in anymore, I observed. I rode on. A freshly ploughed field on the right rose up in the sun like a pink powderpuff. An archway smiled.

'Who owns the estate?' I asked at the hotel down the road.

'That's Garmon's Estate' was the reply. 'Sir John Cotrell.'

'What does he do?'

'Oh, he's involved in many things…'

'Will I get to Hay eventually?'

'Oh yes - eventually.'

There was a beautiful church on the hillside, cone-capped. There were fruit trees in the foreground. A man, I thought was a scarecrow, was spraying. There was a small forest of clipped apple trees, picketed, pricketed - lovely, orderly, ghastly! Polythene-sheeted fields billowed and waved like the sea.

A great edifice ahead I thought must be a Victorian hospital? A public school? A convent? Gothic grandeur gone mad! There were jutting gables, conical towers and chimneys enough to swallow all the coal in Wales. This nightmare of red brick at Staunton was the dream of one Jarvis, an eighteenth century leather merchant who, a lady at the church said, didn't want his money to go into property but, by some means, interest accrued on his capital by such vast amounts that this whole enterprise for the education of young men from the village was set up; but there weren't enough young men to sustain it. Not enough staff either, I thought. You'd need a hundred women to keep it clean. Almshouses and a primary school were attached. Part was used as a Youth Hostel. There were all the usual Victorian conglomerate stables and gardens with trees round the back. 'On moonlit nights it's quite macabre' the lady said. Jarvis had wanted to do something, in an improving way, for his home village - hence the diversion of funds, helped, I found out later, by the Bishop of Hereford.

'Hay B4352: nine miles. Brobury 1. Bredwardine $1^1/_2$' I celebrated with a Mars bar - and a leak.

There were all the right things at Bredwardine: a stud of Welsh cobs; a vicarage on the Brobury side of the zig-zag bridge, where Kilvert might have courted his wife; lambs playing on the rutted, crumbling banks, soil running from their feet and showering down to the river shimmering below; dappled fields; pear and apple blossom; mistletoe; a kestrel floating and turning swiftly in the air. The Wye, here, is like the Severn at Eyton, near Shrewsbury; the same sandy banks, eroded; the same enduring bridges, farms, fields; horsey country. Pear blossom in front of a farmhouse surprises you as you mount the bridge on the turn. The banks are lined with willow and alder. Outstanding, of course, are the horse chestnuts, leafing out. A Welsh mountain pony is tucked away with a group of inquisitive lambs in a gully, where a feeder stream enters the Wye. A yellow hammer poses, crested, on a hedge, besotted with the sun.

The church, just off the road, tells you a lot about the eighteenth century: cold and enduring. You think of Kilvert with his new bride, returning in a carriage from his honeymoon, the happy villagers lining the drive up to the vicarage next to the church. You realise from his portrait in the church what a handsome man he was. The ultimate Victorian parson; a figure to be looked up to; adored by young and old alike. That portrait takes your mind off the rest of the church whose outward leaning, grey stone walls suggest that it might have been like a prison to him.

Now, here is a lucky find! A tablet on the north wall *'To the memory of George Jarvis Esq, munificent benefactor of three parishes, Bredwardine, Staunton and Letton. The poor of this parish, grateful for the liberal provision bequeathed to them by his last will, have caused this monument to be erected out of the ample fund, appropriated to their use under the direction of the Rt. Rev. Foliat Herbert Walker Cornwall, Lord Bishop of Hereford...1804.'* Ah!!

You look back at the bearded cleric, elbow on octagonal table, book in hand, seated on fine chair, his legs easily spread, his coat beautifully cut, his shoes nicely styled, and you think isn't it fitting that today the scribbling diarist is more famous than Jarvis, the Lord Bishop of Hereford, or Sir Geo. Cornwall, Bart, his brother, and another Governor of the Trust?

Outside, under a churchyard yew, you sit on Kilvert's table tomb, while more gladsome yellow hammers play about, a man feeds the sheep, fish and wild duck leap, rotten trees sink to a watery sleep... You can't quote Kilvert, but you can quote Gray: *'One morn I missed him on the customed hill.../The next with dirges due in sad array/Slow through the church way path we saw him borne.'*

Some people long to see the Pyramids, the Grand Canyon, the Taj Mahal, I wanted to see the source of the Wye. I had left Townsend in his shed at Aberystwyth, given him the day off, and taken a bus to Ponterwyd. You know you have arrived at Ponterwyd when you see the George Borrow Hotel. 'Enjoy yourself' said the friendly bus driver. He was, I think, puzzled that I could enjoy myself by myself in this way. (Perhaps he knew what a task I had set myself, but did not want to spoil the child-like expression he could see on my face.) Somewhere on Pumlumon (Plynlimon), 2468 feet up, the Severn and Wye rise like twins within a matter of yards of one another. Borrow writes of 'possessing' the source of the Severn and the Wye, so urgent was his desire to see it.

Along the A44 road, familiar to me from countless motorbike trips in my youth, past the Central Generating Board (the Rheidol or its tributary is harnessed from its infancy) old mine works, old shells of wheel houses - a scarred landscape. I thumbed a lift. Apparently motorists don't like my 'terrorist' plastic bag in which I keep apples and Mars bars, but a lorry driver stopped, 'glad', he said, 'of the company.' I will call him the man from Hull. He was returning to that distant port after delivering caravans to - you guessed it - Aberystwyth. Larkin and Wilberforce came into the conversation, but, seeing Llangurig only a few miles to the east and the road going downhill fast, I begged to be put down.

He went bumping along to Hull and I struck across the marshy fields, across the river to what I thought were signs of life in the forest beyond. I crawled under sheep wire, clambered over bog, heather and sedge. I stumbled upstream to find a stony crossing place. The twelve tribes of Israel could have crossed there, but they would have caught their flowing robes in the fence. I trailed one foot in the water, spiked my shins on fir and larch, falling about to gain the forest road. 'Is there anybody there' I called. I suddenly doubted if I'd see any more signs of life; the forestry workers had all gone deep to work. There was a van ahead and I fell in with Denis, the timber haulier. He had a lorry such as the twelve tribes could have put all their possessions on; the height of the cab was dizzying; the power in that engine, the load of timber, gargantuan. So far as I could tell, above the roar of diesel, he was taking me to Bennet Evans' farm, where the path went direct to the source of the Wye. He dropped me on the roadside, at the farm entrance. Well, I made a rather unpractised, clumsy descent. (There were only two steps down from the cab seat, which was about fifteen feet from the ground, and there was a chain-saw in between.) I landed on my back on the track, dusted myself off as if nothing had happened, and wished Denis good day.

Just by the farm house a pick-up pulled up, two collie dogs in the back aching to get at me. Shepherd Maldwyn (everybody tells you their name) assured me 'it is only two and a half miles by the path, a bridge, a few old barns…' Streams flow everywhere. It is treacherous terrain: string, barbed wire, improvised fencing and gates, the bodies of sheep, litter the road or the river running by. There is a weather station, a measuring gauge (one foot, the river seems to be); a goldfinch skips from post to post ahead, the river thins. It is tiny, but tumbling tumultuously. There is silence and cacophony in the same breath. Lambs spurt from under foot. It is exciting looking for the birth of a river at the time of lambs. There are more sheep pens, dips, folds, tubular bars - all the paraphernalia of a shepherd's life - ranged over unlimited acres of these inhospitable hills. Everything stretches to the horizon - and beyond. 'Two and a half miles!'

I came to a second bridge, a third, a fourth; hay barns; sheep cratches; a spare tractor or two; a caravan. What I thought at first was a sheep dip was a disinfectant tank. Disease prevention. Tenuous lateral streams threaded through rocky laybys, shallow, horseshoe shaped. The river was stronger than I. Men know where the source is, or think they know, but they have never been - like men who know about gold… The little elusive chuckle of baby riverhood disappeared before my ears and eyes. Gold goes beyond men's grasp. I lurched and lunged through the mountain sponge. 'Two and a half miles…right against the forest fence.' Maldwyn's very words! I could die up here, I thought. I see why men take helicopters. I stomped my way by little paths stitched into the mountainside; each an old sheep's Threadneedle Street. The sun came round into position for my last picture; my last memorial. My reward for all that effort. Like being presented by nature with your baccalaureat.

Everything got smaller, more constricted by rocks, rushes, the rank rawness of it all; the struggle to be born, the struggle to survive. I stepped onto rocks hemming in the river, not doubting they would hold – they have held for some millennia. A ewe on a hummock looked up to study me, cocking her head. Daylight and the river dwindled by. The sun was already creeping down the afternoon sky. I could step across the river here, play with him like a baby. Or is it a she? What's a nice girl like you doing here?

Talk about waterfalls! This is the finest spectacle on earth; a continuously unravelling ribbon of beauty. The rock deepens as the river straightens from its parturition point down through, yes, a series of hatches perfectly placed by Mother Nature, the oldest model engineer! It doesn't really straighten out; you only think and hope it will. The struggle of death is nothing to the struggle of being born. Poets learned this from the rivers. Sheep prove it here every day. A one foot bend – all this water going through a passage of rock one foot wide to feed Birmingham! High on the rushy slope frog spawn, like ground rice or tapioca, scums the grass. Jellied hills. The baby river, gone into hiding again, is swaddled in rushes, in the bosom of the hills. Under the stern brow of the mountain, it is cushioned by sphagnum moss.

Slurp, slurp… I drank from the tiny orifice. It was like a manager, in a cave. The baby smiled. In advance of all that restlessness, it was quite still! There is a cairn at the top, and a slab of slate with a mysterious arrow and 1865 engraved on it. Listen. Another baby stream. A playground of baby streams. One of them, tumbling down the far side of the mountain, is the Severn. Would I ever find the road? Any road? Mine went westward. Maldwyn didn't tell me I should cross the Severn. He wouldn't think of that. Crossing a fresh river is an everyday experience for him. 'PLEASE SHUT THE GATE.' By the farm, I emerged on the Aberystwyth road at Eisteddfa Gurig, five miles east of where I should have been. A boy from Sheffield University picked me up in his green mini van. 'Going to see a friend at Aber.' Boy did he drive!

Elan taking advantage of the welcome sign!

Turning our backs on Wales for the present, we will hole up in Shropshire; for those of us lucky enough to have been born there the heartland of England, if not the centre of the universe. Shropshire is one of the world's best-kept secrets. The average Englishman probably knows more about Benidorm, Ibiza or Hong Kong than he does about this, one of the largest of England's inland counties. Landlocked, Shropshire has been, as it were, pickled in obscurity. It is 'on the road to nowhere.' No charter plane brings tourists to the Long Mynd. Only in quite recent years has a motorway (the M54) partly bisected the eastern more industrial half of the county, to the greater advantage of Telford than Shrewsbury, the county town. Thomas Telford's A5 has run through for over a century, linking London with Wales and with Ireland via Holyhead. Telford was a master of viaducts and short-cuts and no respecter of Shropshire's hills which, however, more than any other physical feature, have led to her preservation, sealing and hemming her in. Shaped like a round-backed bear, she sits with her front and hind paws prodding Wales. Cheshire, to the north, consorts with Liverpool; Stafford boasts closer connections with the Black Country, with more brass and beer; Hereford and Worcester, to the south, have redder, sandier acres, more splendid cattle and pottery, not to mention cathedrals; Wales, to the west, is prying, prattling, and best kept at a distance. Shropshire keeps its shutters up.

Shrewsbury, the administrative centre of the county, sits aloof on a hill, almost circled by the Severn and linked to the outside world by two main bridges, one of which is named in Welsh the other the English. It suffers wet feet when the river floods. It has been much knocked about, but smiles through its injuries. It has a hill named Pride. At the Mount, outside the Welsh Bridge, Darwin was born. Many famous men have passed through its school. Kings and princes have passed through its gates. Its pride is justified. Shropshire, being a mainly agricultural county, has no inclination to draw attention to itself, and Shrewsbury – a true county town – no need to shout her wares.

Shropshire, then, is no amoeba-like blob on the map, but a solid bear whose tough skin is stretched over a stout, skeletal framework of hills. It squats, stand-offishly, thrusting here and there a paw into Wales or poking it with its snout. Its sternum and rib-cage are the border hills, with a reinforced breastplate, Offa's Dyke; its haunches are the South Shropshire hills; it has a hump, the Wrekin, on its back. It has known war and baiting, but it now sits picking fleas off itself in the sun. It is among the proudest survivors of history. Shropshire covers 1,348 square miles; its highest hills, the Clee and the Wrekin, are true mountains, well over a thousand feet; its greatest river, the Severn, once flowed northwards like the Dee, but, after the Ice Age, broke through a gap near Coalbrookdale and headed towards Bristol, in the long argument of time, creating a network of international trade through the port of Gloucester and providing Midland men with a highway to the sea. It is no exaggeration to say that Shropshire fuelled the Industrial Revolution and - trade following the flag – created the British Empire. But it is with agriculture that we wish to dwell first; for, stretched and tough as the hide of the old bear is, it is among the most fertile in the world.

'One of the pleasantest things in the world is going on a journey', wrote William Hazlitt, one of Shropshire's greatest sons; *'but'*, he added, *'I like to go by myself.'* He could not see why anyone should want to walk and talk at the same time.

Walking is a journey in the head, an adventure; the wind blows throw your head, your mind and your memories. The landscape is part of your memory; but it is always different because you, at different stages of your life, are different. My feet first saw the light at Lady Forester's Hospital, Much Wenlock, on the morning of March 8, 1927. No doubt my little pink toes were carefully examined to see if they were all there. I intend to take them back and present them, I hope in good order, nearer my seventieth birthday – Dreadnought boots and all. Next to riding a horse – which requires hard leg-work and is hazardous on roads these days – walking is the best way of seeing Shropshire. And not just walking. Climbing, I mean. Stand in the low-lying lanes and fields of my cousin's farm at Eyton, Baschurch, and you can see almost all the hills of Shropshire like the rim of a great terracotta bowl around you. Stand on any one of those hills, especially in May, and you see that the bowl is filled with cream.

'Abraham was a framer', one of my boys at school once wrote, with a nice, unconscious adjustment of the truth. If our forefather Abraham had not left Ur to travel to Canaan, our heritage would not have been the same. He, with a little assistance from divine intervention, helped to frame it. He was a fixer of sorts. Abraham Darby of Coalbrookdale was a 'framer' too;

and, as we shall see, bent a little to the will of God, nicely, if unconsciously, adjusting our landscape and heritage in the process.

The first Darby that we know anything about at all is John, a seventeenth century nail-maker from Wren's Nest, Dudley, who was probably the owner of a field or two, a few sheep or cattle and a horse to ply his trade. It is important to keep this interest in the land and farming in mind from the outset. Iron working was a flourishing trade, but land represented a visible and tangible asset. The first Darby to come to Coalbrookdale was Abraham I, via Bristol where he had served his apprenticeship in the casting of copper and brass. One suspects that he and his son, Abraham II, were always on the look out for ways of improving their decorative as well as their productive skills. These reached their acme in Abraham III who built the famous iron bridge opened in 1781. It had been long in the building, pieces of it lying in evidence on the riverside, ready for erection, section by section, using only iron pegs to hold it together – no unsightly nuts and bolts. It was a wonderful achievement that the whole world flocked to see, but the cost – estimated at £550 in 1775 – had escalated to £2,737-4s-4d. Abraham Darby III was only thirty-nine when he died in 1789. The early Darbys were generally short-lived, energetic, practical men.

Abraham IV lived long and departed from the family tradition of Quakerism, built the new Anglican church at Coalbrookdale, founded the Literary and Scientific Institution there, diversified into property, and continued to advance in society. The Darbys always had a strong humanitarian streak, espousing the Victorian Anti-Slavery and Teetotal movements, and being active in the Anti-Corn Law League. They took a hand in local politics and became strong Liberals. They adjusted not only our material landscape but our moral one as well. In this the women of the family took no small part. There seems to have been generation after generation of good accountants keeping good order of their finances. They also kept journals, windows through which we may glimpse their private lives. They were good at marrying up. Maternalism seems to have been every bit as powerful in them as materialism. It is a sad irony that in no generation of the family were there more than two sons.

In 1852 Alfred Darby I died aged only forty-five and his widow, Rebecca, moved from Astley Abbots to Little Ness. She lived first at Little Ness House, and, being a woman of enlightenment, energy and vision, she took the village in hand. She was well-connected, not only through the Darbys but also through the Christys, hatters, cotton manufacturers and bankers. She had visible and invisible assets. She spotted a farmhouse at Adcote, part of her estate, which she could turn into a grand residence. At another farm, Red House, was a quarry which would provide all the sandstone needed – to be transported down an incline plane, a practice the Darbys had always followed. At Red House the story of the Davies family really begins.

John and Adeline Davies came from South Shropshire to Red House in the early years of the century; he from Great Lyth, she from Diddlebury. You could not imagine two more unspoilt, out of the way places, which remain so to this day. They reared twelve children, of whom one was my father, Tom. At the age of fifty-five, my grandfather died. In the same year my father and my Uncle John, like many more from the village, went to war. It was 1914.

The war memorial opposite the Red House tells the story of those who served and survived and of those who 'laid down their lives.' One grave in the churchyard records in poignant detail how the body of Maurice Darby, Lieutenant in the Grenadier Guards, 'having lain for four days on the battlefield of Neuve Chapelle was, after a long night search in front of the enemy's lines, recovered and brought home by his uncle George Arthur to be laid at rest on this spot.' He was the grandson of Rebecca, and the only son of the squire, Alfred Darby II. The waste of war and the depression in agriculture saddened and, no doubt, shortened Alfred's life. He died in 1925. Maurice Darby's regimental drum remained on display in Little Ness Church for many years. Frederica, his mother, was a well-known figure in the village up to her death in 1946. Mrs Jessie Hanson, who has done much to give a clear, fair picture of this God-fearing family, points to another sad irony: 'Had Maurice Darby been of the same faith as his grandparents, he would not have been a soldier. After his death his mother Frederica, responding to her earlier Quaker training, went to France giving aid to the soldiers.' How tellingly that word 'responding' is used!

My grandmother died in 1935. A photo of her on the beach at Rhyl in black bombazine and gateau hat, poking the sand with her umbrella, is almost all I know of her. She did well to live so long, I recently remarked to my cousin, her eldest surviving grandson. 'But what did she ever do?' he asked. John, my grandfather, was described in his obituary as one of the best agriculturalists in the district, thorough in everything he undertook. No wonder the Darbys picked him to take charge of the principal farm on the Adcote Estate. Carried on by my Uncle Frank, his son Gordon and grandson Guy, it now comprises the Home Farm, extending to about 600 acres. It is, in this age of set-aside and diversification, thoroughly well farmed, a sight for sore eyes, and the one by which other farms in the area are commonly judged.

It is bounded in the north and east by the River Perry. At its western extent is the Platt Bridge, which, if we can believe Richard Gough, was once the boundary with Wales. *'We have by tradition that there was such enmity between the Britains and Saxons, that the Welshmen accounted all for a lawful prize which they stole from the English'*, he says in his History of Myddle. *'And we have a tradition, that the inhabitants of these neighbouring towns'*, - Ruyton-XI-Towns – *'had in every town, a piece of ground adjoining to their houses, which was moated about with a large ditch, and fenced with a strong ditch fence and pale, wherein they kept their cattle every night, with persons to watch them; and that there was a light-horse-man maintained in every town with a good horse, sword, and spear, who was always ready, upon the least notice to ride straight to the Platt Bridge, there to meet his companions; and if they found any Welshman on this side of the Platt Bridge, and the river of Perry, if they could apprehend him he was sure to be put to death. But if the Welshmen had got over the bridge with stolen cattle, then we have an ancient saying that they would cry, 'Ptroove mine own', for the horsemen durst not follow any further; if they were taken beyond the bridge they were straightway hanged.'* Wild West stuff!

This Perry Ground, as it is still known, has been the scene of work and play for generations of Davieses. The riverside fields were a pleasure beach for children bent on bird-nesting, fishing, tree-climbing, rabbit-hunting, and swimming, of course. They have enchanting names: Foxholes, Yewtree Leasow, Old Ryegrass, Flax Moors, Flower Meadow… My grandfather, coming from the Lyth, meaning slope, must have known the advantages of well-drained sandy loam. I can remember my Uncle Frank telling me that Gordon, his son, had put a great deal of effort into improving the drainage of the lower-lying fields. Good drainage is, after all, the basis of good farming. Fields that smile in the sun must work off the rain. You learn a lot by looking at Red House Farm. The picture speaks for itself. You would almost think there were no snags. The operators of other going-concerns will tell you otherwise.

It is well known that after the second world war, responding to government encouragement, British farming increased production and prospered for the first time this century. It is equally well known that the subsequent over-production brought restrictions imposed by the European Common Agricultural Policy which have left many farmers bewildered and discouraged, with sons less eager to follow in their footsteps because the future is so confused. If increase and improvement go together, it is logical – they are entitled to argue – that a very disagreeable future lies ahead. DIG FOR VICTORY and BACKS TO THE LAND were easy slogans to follow during the war. Subsequent farm Ministers have been less inspiring, seeming to be out of touch with reality and too caught up in Common Market concerns. The pattern of farming, I discovered, is constantly changing. To call it kaleidoscopic would be old-fashioned. It is like a fast computer game, flashing imperatives and, just as you are up with the newest alternative idea, moving on. The only thing constant is the question: 'What next?' Or 'Whatever next?'

I was to hit Haughmond at the time of bluebells, a place I had not known as a child, but near my birthplace – and the birthplace of industry, Coalbrookdale. It was a thought that unsettled me somewhat. We grow in years – less in strength or opportunity to reach – even when fortune condescends; but something in my bones told me that I would do this. There are times in life when the heart must overrule the head.

Haughmond, with its old, hard-headed hill of pre-Cambrian 'grey whackey' rock, seemed the ideal starting point; Charles Teece, my ideal companion. Training his binoculars on every unsuspecting early bird, we set off through misty bluebell woods, through an avenue of beeches and over fields following the buzzard sign of The Shropshire Way, downhill to the A5 at Atcham. At Attingham bridge over the Tern, we stopped and marvelled at the view of the Park and the happy little river running on to join the Severn nearby. The inscription on the central commemoration plaque, once so bold and clear-cut, is now intriguingly faint. Glasses would not help. We traced the lettering with our fingers, like blind men reading Braille. 'This bridge', it says, 'was erected at the expense of the County AD

MDCCLXXX and decorated at the Expense of Lord Hill Esq. William Hayward Architect.'

How many people stop to read these runic documents now? How many, even in the days of slow coach travel, ever did? I love them. They test your knowledge of Roman numerals. They link you with a nearer, more decorative, elegant age. Suddenly, listening to the timeless call of the pewit, curlew and cuckoo, you realise that you are standing on the same earth as Hill and Hayward – Telford, Capability Brown, John Wesley and Abraham Darby, too – shoulder to shoulder watching the same river and marvelling at the power and properties of water and our command of it.

Ignoring the Romans at Wroxeter, we struck left to Eaton Constantine, past prime potato fields using, Charles said, the 'bed system' of planting and newly chatted beet seedlings couched in pink counterpanes of sun-warmed loam. The farmer was 'footing' the earth, walking his ground and inspecting the progress of his crops, timing in his head to a nicety the next need to spray and revelling like us in the sheer fresh beauty of tilth in spring. Even dandelions by the roadside looked new-born, happy and healthy as the lambs round Garmston and Buildwas where the riverside fields are given over to pasture.

'Look at those lambs, stretching to the sun', I said.

'They're growing', said Charles, 'so fast that their skins are almost too tight!'

Where the Severn meanders almost to a standstill beyond Leighton, we found a sandy beach by the river. 'Better than the beach at Rhyl', we declared in unison. Slinging off our rucksacks, we sat down and shared out our sandwiches, cake, apples, pears and Mars bars. The river yawned open-mouthed in its wide-open bed. The sand banks the far side were pitted with what looked like old sand martins' nests. About thirty yearling cross-Hereford bullocks paraded on the ledges trampled, no doubt, by many generations of their kind: one of the most typical Severnside scenes. The silence was palpable. Lazy cattle, lazy river, lazy noon-time air – and even lazier men.

'We'll make Ironbridge', I avowed, sighting the quartet of cooling towers, vapourless and inert. Passing Ironbridge National Power Station, we put on speed, to get off the busy road and onto the Severnside path. We fell in with about thirty young rambling humans, all in single file, where the path threads through a wilderness of fast-growing nettles, dandelions, docks and scrub willow. Jubilee Gardens were brilliant with pansies, cherry blossom and the first breath-taking reminder that lilac, like may, ranks as a princess, whatever the claims of the horse-chestnut and beech to be as royal as the oak in the courtly days of spring.

On the outskirts of Ironbridge the fields sprawl, tame and flat with a softer aspect as the sun creeps round to the south, softening the outlines of the flat-bellied cooling towers, and drawing the people out of their houses (public and private) down through their gardens to the riverside walk, drifted with poplar cotton and the warm smell of beer. Nature is now smartened up for the tourist. A large, lazy cabin-cruiser bright with red, blue and white, dawdled and dreamed upstream while a frog displayed a perfect leg-kick as he mastered this huge watercourse, on his way where downstream – a few more yards ahead, or all the way to the Bristol Channel? 'Perhaps he's a transatlantic frog', I said. Past the pumping station and the nineteenth century span of the ever-widening river, you catch echoes of charcoal burners and smoke in the steep sides of the valley, still thickly wooded with self-renewing oaks where, Charles suggested, nightingales would be happy to sing. There is an eeriness about this approach to the 'town' – remembering that when industry first came here it must have seemed like world's end. In spite of the concourse of people that you know tramp over and around the Bridge, in and out of six or seven far-flung museums, and umpteen tightly packed cafes and souvenir shops, there is a sweet silence down on the riverside path, reflecting the silence and somnolence of the river itself.

Then you get an 'eyeful' of the Bridge – as Abraham Darby intended that you should. It was built as an advertisement of his powers as an iron-master, a piece of overweening exhibitionism. It yawns, open-mouthed over the mulligatawny soup below. No need to 'finger' its inscription; it is a super-subscription painted in white capitals on the great semi-circular arch: AD MDCCLXXIX (1779 – exactly one year older than the stone bridge at Attingham). Charles and I marvelled afresh at the solidity and airiness of it, straddling like a Colossus the river, declared 'DANGEROUS' on notices along the bank. The confidence of the men who built it, the first of its kind in the world!

'And the accuracy!' declared Charles.

'And the endurance', I added, thinking not only of the bridge but also of the men.

And then you think of the men who died in all such undertakings. We proceeded to re-examine the Table of Tolls

	s.	d.
For every time they pass over the Bridge		
For every Coach, Landau, Hearse, Chaise,		
Chair or such like	2.	0
Carriages drawn by Six horses, Mares		
Geldings or Mules	1.	6
Ditto by four	1.	6
For a Calf, pig, sheep or lamb		$0\frac{1}{2}$
For every Foot Passenger going over the Bridge		$0\frac{1}{2}$

A herd of young Mercian cows watch me pass by.

I was looking for an out-of-the-way place to write, without friends to distract me, but sufficiently near what I call the industrial East to help correct the wholly agricultural picture of Shropshire formed since my youth. Leighton Home Farm had been described to me as 'pure Kate Greenaway'. It is near Much Wenlock, near Ironbridge and Coalbrookdale, just up the road from Buildwas – famous for its abbey and power station. Mrs Rickards, who rents the house, put no impediments in my way. I could come and go as I liked. There were conveniences all over the house. I didn't want meals; they were a waste of a daylight traveller's time.

Bruce Chatwin would have made a marvellous job of describing Home Farm. There were flowers everywhere; it is timbered within and without; japonica clasped the long front, matching the old red brick with its clusters of carmine flowers, cupped in glossy 'apple-green' leaves. Length seems to have been a passion with farmhouse architects in the eighteenth and nineteenth centuries. This house, not particularly high, is as long as a cricket pitch. It is part of the Leighton Estate, centred on Leighton Hall, at the heart of this point-to-point racing community. You expect to see long stable-blocks with picturesque clock-towers sounding the hours; long, gated driveways obscured by rhododendrons, which lead to lawns and borders once tended by a small army of gardeners, to coach-houses smelling of Stockholm tar and harness oil; to boot-rooms and gun-rooms, cellars and glasshouses, cold-frames and melon beds; orchards and kitchen gardens; an arboretum, perhaps. The odd Wellintonia or monkey-puzzle tree still commands the scene. Whatever its origins, Home Farm House, two rooms deep and a chain in length, with its two staircases – one at the far end for the domestics and the men – was now my base. Its handsome front door, repainted and weathered over the years, has acquired the soft smile of a summer cloud. Is it grey? Is it blue? I drew the curtains of my room to make sure I did not miss the birdsong and the early morning light. It was silent all night except for the occasional 'flap', as if someone impatiently closed a book and threw it away. It was not Bruce Chatwin's ghost! There were a hundred or more books in the passage by my room, but they were all packed tightly on their shelves. In the morning, through the parting in the curtains, I saw the jackdaws sweep busily from the corner of the gable, to-ing and fro-ing and wasting no time. I was up and away.

You say it quickly: Wigwig. Heading for Much Wenlock from Shrewsbury you pass the turn at the bottom of Harley Bank. I doubt if one in a hundred motorists, putting on speed past the Feathers Inn, even sees the name

– or if he does, thinks twice. I came down the hill, a passenger in a friend's car, many years ago. The corners had, even then, been blunted. My friend's Daimler coasted down without alarm. Another friend, a lady, cushioned at the back, began to recount the story of the farmer from Wig Wig, who, drunk, drove down there with his passenger, the schoolmaster, in his pony-trap, crashed into a telegraph pole, killing pony and passenger – he being thrown clear over the hedge to a soft landing in a field. 'Fancy', said my friend the driver, not taking his eyes off the road. The Daimler made no sound. The lady, fresh from a shopping trip to Wolverhampton, thought no more of it, purred over her purchases, and pointed to the view. She did not know that the farmer was my father.

Yes, I knew the story. I knew the turn and, opposite the church on the hill where we children of Mad Tom were christened. Say it quickly: Wig Wig. It means what it says: two farms. (Actually, there are three; two on an estate, and one by the ford, but set back, almost out of sight, on – or is it in – the river; Mill Farm.) Beyond, as the sign informs you, is a settlement named Homer – but let that pass; it is modern and of no consequence to me. If I had not gone to Leighton, I might never have gone to Wig Wig – such is the topsi-turviness of life. Mary told me that, coming from the Shrewsbury road, she sometimes takes the turn to Wig Wig and Homer because it saves her car the long haul up to Wenlock Edge, that is Harley Bank. The road comes out on the Leighton side, where it is signed: Home and Wig Wig. It was from there that I decided to make my search. It proved a revelation.

Homer is, indeed, quite a populous place with much new housing devel-opment. There, among the clean white-faced bungalows and Mon Repos, I spotted a farm. It had the necessary evidence of life: a Land Rover drawn up by the door. A gentleman came out of the house. 'Wig Wig? Go on down. You might see Tony Downes. He, or his wife will know. They go back a long way.' They do indeed – but not that far. 'See
Mrs Brassington, she's been here all her life', they said. I found Mrs Brassington in her bungalow. She asked me in. 'Cup of tea?' She apologised for her difficulty in straightening up. 'Kidney trouble.' Her son and two lovely grandchildren were with her. Andrew, aged four, informed me he would soon be going to school. Sarah, a little older, was already there. They had rosy cheeks and smiles, such as children used to have. Nothing puts you so much at ease as naturalness in children. I thought if I had teeth like Andrew's. I too would smile – and take life as it comes.

'Oh, I remember your father', said Mrs Brassington, coming in with the tea. 'Tall, well set-up. Liked a drop to drink. And your mother – a little lady.

Played the piano. I remember them clearly, though I'd be only about six – the age of Sarah here. Your dad was a character! Mad Tom, we called him. The policeman – he's dead now, so it doesn't matter me telling you – told me how your dad drove the pony and trap after him up the market steps in Shrewsbury – the policeman couldn't stop him.'

Her son asked if he was the one who drove the pony through the flooded brook and drowned.

'No, that was Mad Jack'.

Philip, Mrs Brassington's other son, then came in; he was working at Mill Farm and offered to take me down. I took my leave of kind Mrs Brassington, Andrew and the children, and went with Philip in his pick-up and trailer, slopping through the ford. Hedges there stood high above the banks which towered above the roof of the pick-up. One false move and you might, if you were lucky, end up in a field. Suddenly, by unorthodox switch-back, Philip turned back on himself, trailer rocking, headed down to the brook, drove over a makeshift bridge and pulled up at a barn. A man appeared at the door.

'Is he the farmer' I asked.

'He's a partner.'

I was less certain than ever who lived there now. The house looked like a small left-over irrelevance, compared with the range of barns, stockyards, machines and implements about the place. I was also less sure of my grounds for being there. Philip and partner are new-style operators, none of whose business my father would have recognised – and I certainly didn't. I thanked him for his trouble and he pointed me towards Red House Farm and the road that would lead me eventually, by Harley Bank – a hard slog – back to Leighton.

Only Mrs Brassington really understands, I told myself. She was probably christened at Harley Church herself. The rector had not answered my letter in which I asked if I might see the baptismal register, though I sent a stamped, addressed envelope. Born in 1920, Mrs Brassington was just able to remember my parents at the Wig Wig. And, just able to remember, she was just able to understand.

'In my end is my beginning', I chanted to the Housman-haunted heights of Wenlock Edge. *'Hereux qui, comme Ullysse, a fait un beau voyage….'* I was hurrying on to my appointment with Mrs Reynolds, the matron at Lady Forester's Hospital, somewhere along the Sheinton road. When I wrote to her earlier in the year asking if I might visit my birthplace, I did mention that I had a good pair of feet.

Mrs Reynolds and her lovely team of nurses welcomed their unusually healthy visitor, showed me round the old maternity ward, sluice room, laundry, labour ward, the doctors' room, nurses' quarters etc., all very little altered since mother hastened there from the Wig Wig for the birth of her first child in 1925 (early in the morning of October 19) and even more speedily on two successive occasions at even smaller, less convenient hours. I saw the silver trowel with which Lady Forester laid the foundation stone in 1903. Olwen Yeats, one of several nurses who seemed to be natives of Much Wenlock and to have worked there for many years, shared with me her evident pleasure in chatting and attending to the silver-haired residents. (It is now a community nursing home.) She said, laughing, that she might be related by marriage to W B Yeats, but she did not know much of his poetry apart from *'tread softly, because you tread on my dreams'*.

I was shown the register of births, clearly stating that my twin sister and I were delivered at 5.10 and 5.20 a.m. respectively and that we were 'healthy'.

'You look very healthy', said Mrs Reynolds, noticing my brick-red fore-head, the skin taut as the iron brown of Abraham Darby's bridge.

'Good for a bit longer', I thought, but did not wish to dwell.

'I hope you have not been disappointed', she said as I left.

'Far from it', I replied, 'it was a pleasure just to be admitted.'

Within two myles, there is a famous thing, cal'de Offa's dyke, that reacheth farre in length.

Thomas Churchyard *Worthies of Wales, 1587*

The best time to walk on Offa's Dyke is spring or early summer, and when you are nearer seventeen than seventy. I did it when I was nearly sixty five.

On June 7th, 1991, I found myself at Buttington, just south of Llanymynech, following the sign: LLYBR CLAWDD, OFFA'S DYKE. At 9.30 in the morning, I felt like an old Offa. The shrill alarm of an approaching diesel train kept me on my toes, crossing the familiar Shrewsbury to Aberystwyth line. The black and white timbered belfry of Buttington church, so characteristic of this area, smiled over the wheat field through which I passed, even over the Site of Offa's Dyke Business Park, on the road marked Holiday Route, which I crossed before scaling Long Mountain. Goldfinches played in the fields of seeding grasses ahead. Soft barley heads stroked my arm. I felt at one with the thousands who had, over the ages, passed this way.

'Blessings on all good people who go about putting yellow arrows and white acorn signs on the posts for the benefit of dreamers like me,' I sang. 'Feel no more the heat of the sun,' I crooned. The wind was from the north-west. I would not sweat.

I met a youth who told me that the man at the cottage on the hill-side ahead of me had done the whole Offa's Dyke walk, each way, twice. Cows, slumped on a steep sunny slope of their meadow, looked as if they did not care for such exertion. A farm, deserted even by dogs, strewn with old, worn-out vans and machinery, and paved to the door with sharp-edged shale, suggested that you had to be feckless as well as tough to live up here. The gate-ways were troughs of liquid mud after the storms of May, but admission was free. It was Monday, Welshpool market day. The folks were in town. I had the world to myself.

From Buttington View (B&B, 250m.) the path went up into the sky. Was that a raven perched on a post by a parcel of land growing raspberries? A chaffinch – always my constant companion on walks like this – sang his heart out, achingly, as if he needed oil. The hill and rutted fields hurt my feet, till I reached a lane, grassy in the middle and edged with stitchwort, ferns, cow-parsley, campion and clover. The river behind me shone like a silver lake. Powys Castle commanded the stage beyond that, dwarfing, thank goodness, the modern development in and around Welshpool.

A great ash towered beside me, 'feathering' into leaf. Mighty Offa's mighty oaks were already fully fledged. Sheep in a meadow to my left indicated I was nearing another farm – my cousin Bob's, maybe. Larks trilled. The land was opening out. What was the name given to the topsoil hereabouts? Head. The Breidden and all the other dolerite hills are capped like an offending county council, but Long Mountain is blessed with a good foot of remarkably rich agricultural earth.

I stepped off the Dyke for two reasons: one, to visit my cousins Bob and Edie Morris at Long Mountain Farm; the other, to see Trelystan Church. Bob, in his seventies, had just given up riding and training racehorses, but still carries on with the hundred and one other things you do on a farm. Edie keeps a good table, and in the spring her house is a nursery for every kind of garden plant imaginable; seed potatoes in dark corners spurt passively, awaiting burial before resurrection from the ground; geraniums 'finger' the warm kitchen air; dozens of seedlings are pricked out in trays on the window-sill above the sink. It is like a miniature Kew. Everything at Long Mountain is well looked after, including me. I am there to rest, take in nutrients, spurt passively, and – like the trailing geraniums – take off at will.

I decided on a small detour to Trelystan where there is a remarkable church. Black and white, it is not quite so perilously situated as Melverley, and probably not quite so old; but it is romantically set in fields with sheep that lie about the lane and hardly stir when you pass. It is a world's-end sort of place, crouching among yews and plantations of spruce which shelter it, as they do the lonely farmsteads in the vicinity. More intriguing even than the church, is the little log-cabin church hall. Externally, it is 'clad' in vertical, not horizontal pine logs. It is very low and long, like the church; it too has a slate roof. Both receive optimum light from a multitude of small windows. In the church hall, you can see, by looking through the window, trestle tables covered with white cloths, ready, it seems, for a feast. You know you are in Wales when you see such signs of communal hospitality. The Church of England does not ordinarily act like this. You can, looking in on a bare room, almost see the little Welsh women bustling about, with tea-urns steaming in the kitchen at the back, sandwiches cut in triangles and piled on plates, cakes coconut iced, and Victoria sponges powdered on top and yawning with jam and cream. Who are they doing it for? The Unexpected or the One Expected Guest? Are they perhaps entertaining angels unawares?

The church, regrettably, is locked. No matter, I have been in before. Through the many windows – diamond-leaded and all set at a convenient height – you can view the interior from outside. Even externally, you notice, all the timbers are pegged in the proper fashion. There is no satanic iron here – except on the door handles and hinges and the occasional pointless hook. Wood is the primary material, functional and ornate. There is a screen opposite the pulpit which is said to have come from Chirbury Abbey at the time of the Dissolution. Some of the timbers in the vestry, a notice informs you, date from the thirteenth century. Wood, when it gets to that age, is more powerful than stone. Leaving the churchyard – in which, you notice, there is a comfortable amount of room – by way of the small gate behind the church hall, you see that even the window over the ladies' kitchen is made in the shape of a wooden cross.

I left Trelystan optimistically, to the sound of curlew 'voicing' invisibly over the valley – a sound which is so immediately recognisable, but impossible to describe. A buzzard perched on a telephone pole, unaware of me or the true purpose of the pole. A ewe shuffled out of my path, dragging her dirty bottom behind her. 'You want to get yourself cleaned up', I told her. She looked at me as I were a twentieth century fool who didn't understand the properties of unwashed wool. Life on a mountain can be hard at the best of times. 'Food, shelter and clothing', I rehearsed to myself, 'are all we need – basically.' But I had the best of both worlds: to the spiritual welcome I felt at Trelystan was added the material hospitality of Long Mountain Farm.

Re-orientating myself, I set out next morning for Forden, through woods of storm-lashed sycamore and larch, by flooded – and sometimes redirected – paths, smelling sweetly of bracken, still damp from the recent heavy rains. Sun reawakened the crushed memories of childhood, lighting up mossy stowls and pit-prop piles – the age-old mark of worked woods. My feet stirred the leaf-litter of millennia. I half expected to hear a turtle-dove.

At Greenwood Lodge, I crossed the Forden road. On the next section of the Dyke, I thought I saw ahead of me a man, leaning against a tree. He had bright yellow hair and theatrical red and blue clothes. I had met no one till now. He was like someone out of Oklahoma. Should I sing 'Oh, what a beautiful morning', or ask him for a light? Then I noticed he was losing straw from under his rain-soaked hat. He was no Curly, but a straight scarecrow.

In this Rip-Van-Winkle no-man's-land between Montgomery and Bishop's Castle, you are as surprised to hear peacocks – a new sound of the countryside – as you are to hear cows being called for milking. The latter at least gives you an idea of the time. After crossing the Camlad, whose steep banks were well-trodden by cattle, I came to a line of deserted cottages, out of sight of any road but fronted by a grassy, level part of the Dyke which must have been the playground of many farm-workers' children in the past. A butterfly, perhaps a painted lady, and a yellow hammer jaunted ahead. A cock pheasant was dust-bathing in the side of the Dyke which ran in a clear line to Little Brompton Farm. The high standing barley was ripening fast. The many goodly oaks added aptness to the acorn sign. Two shire horses stood under one, sensibly drowsing while I walked on. At the 'Ditches', cows stared at me with some concern. A sign-post said Churchstoke 1, Bishops Castle 6, Kerry 7. At five o'clock I was still half-way to nowhere. I put my faith in the road – not looking hard for the path; but I could see the dyke to my right, to the west. At seven o'clock, I booked in at the Old Times Guest House, Bishops Castle, 'phoned my friend Syd Blakemore to say I would see him later, had a bath and relaxed. It was just the place for an old timer like me.

Bishops Castle is a strange little ragamuffin town which used to have forty-two pubs. (Drovers had thirsts.) It has a Victorian red-brick bank with swallows in the eaves and jackdaws in the chimneys. The market clock sounds every hour, day and night. The streets run mostly up. Syd, who lives at Bank Head, is one of my oldest friends; he sat for years next to me in class at the Priory and is still one of those special people who know where they belong and are always there when you call. He took me, next morning, to Crow's Nest, where I rejoined the Offa's Dyke path.

The fifteen miles to Knighton are, I think, the best part of this 'out-of-this-world' walk. Over Edenhope (Ed'n'op) Hill the may blossom moved thrushes to sing. Sheep constantly called from hill to hill on either side of the valley, reminding me of Corvedale. Shorn ewes seemed to be grieving, not for the loss of their wool, but for the loss of their lambs, suffering more than a temporary separation. Curlews called in the same melancholy key. I talked to a woman hanging out washing at a farm. 'Be sure you see Mainstone church', she said. Foxgloves and campion attracted bees by the roadside. The churchyard contained the graves of many Davieses. The church itself was a cool resting place – and obviously the haunt of bats.

'Beautiful here in the winter', said a roadman from his parked pick-up on the hill beyond the church.

'Not for the farmer', I suggested, spotting a farmhouse half-hidden in the coomb.

'Forty poun' for a cow, eight poun' for a sheep – oh, I wouldna mind being a farmer 'ere!'

Ceri Forest ahead. Ah, the roadman, who worked for the Shropshire County Council, would only have to repair a few holes in that short stretch of the hill. After that it was the responsibility of Powys C.C.

Cwm Farm, its fantails and hens with feathered feet, was for sale. This was a secret world where even bluebells seemed to have mistaken the time for blooming, or stayed out late. I regained the Dyke, double now – one major, one minor, running parallel. There was a huge drop to the west. I lunched in a bower of wild roses. Sheep in the valley must have numbered thousands – as many as in the cast of a Cecil B de Mille epic from the Bible – but there was not a man in sight. I took small, circumspect steps downhill, after lunch, between rows of foxgloves and tree-high hedge roses. At the bottom, I bathed my feet in a stream. Four Charolais bullocks, overcome by curiosity at my coloured rucksack, snorted and sniffed like hot-air balloons round my back. The bank, undermined on a bend by the force of the water, gave way. The bullocks roared with whatever passes for bovine laughter and rushed away, beside themselves with obstreperous glee.

Back on the high ground of the Dyke, I suddenly realised what a clever fellow old Offa was: he took a natural feature and simply made more of it. Nature is the master in these parts. Offa was just her apprentice, albeit a ready one. I, however, was in a state of complete isolation. Where, I wondered, were all the people who walk the Dyke? There were more acres per skylark up here than anywhere else in Shropshire – if we were in that county at all. Jack Mytton Way. (We had Wild Edric Way.) Where were the horses? I was tempted perversely to leave the path and join the road running tamely below. Only for a moment, however; there was no house in sight; a car went along perhaps once in half an hour.

The path run out in a newly stripped silage field, featureless and brown as autumn. Doubling back to the village of Newcastle, I sought a live, informative soul. There was no one about. At last, after loitering suspiciously too long, a dog barked outside a house, a bedroom window was thrown up and a man in his pyjamas, who was short of breath, told me his wife had gone to Blackpool and that I could go through the farm, cross the silage field and find the dyke path yonder at the top of the hill. Like a wartime infantryman, I was going over the top.

Springfield Farm offered B & B. I would have settled for a nice cup of tea. Through gate after gate, past sheepfold after sheepfold, I struggled on. Badgers had set up whole terraces of homes along this part of the dyke. It was perilously perforated I thought. Would I fall in, never to be seen again? Larks choired celestially. At a lonely farm, a hose-pipe left dribbling into a bucket saved my life. I came to a wood with a stream and a bridge constructed by the Royal Engineers in 1985. A beautiful Welsh black cow stood in the shade of a tree overhanging the stile bearing the regulation acorn sign. Would she allow me to pass? Like a good Samaritan, she moved aside. A steep ascent was followed by the expected descent – but into a quarry. After that I lost the track and headed for a farm which was open to the despised, tame road that I had rejected till now.

At Knighton, Radnorshire, I found no cup of tea. It was after five o'clock. Ice-cream and half a pint of Tetley bitter at a pub - a bad mix – was all I could find. I sat under the clock tower in the square which Housman must have known, and studied the people in cars and on foot rushing to the Convenience Store to buy the evening paper to see what events of the day they had missed. Then I went down to the church, to see how many Knighton lads had died in two wars. I thought of Housman's memorial in Ludlow churchyard:

> *'Goodnight; ensured release*
> *imperishable peace,*
> *Have these for yours…'*

NORTHUMBRIA – AND THE REST

IN March 1998 I was travelling along the Pilgrims Way again – with Titanium, a super-light mountain bike with twenty-three gears – looking to gain access via Gravesend and Tilbury to the road to York. As well as the architectural wonders of this part of England, I wanted to see where Constable's family had set up their mills and boat-building yards and Robert Ransome had developed his method of casting ploughshares in the eighteenth century – a method still used to this day.

Brentwood in Essex was a fine surprise. I found digs easily, within walking distance of the theatre and an Alan Ayckbourn play. 'CHIPS AT McDONALD'S. HOME TO BED', I wrote in my diary.

The next night I spent at Coggeshall, poised to explore the Colne Valley. Cobbett would have called it 'a delightfully pretty town'. Perhaps. It has every kind of house, in every style and shade so long as it be pastel – pink, green, yellow, blue – as decreed by law. East Street teeters on the river's edge. The rest of the town teeters on a hill, topped by a massive church, next to the fifteenth century Woolpack Inn. It is a marvellous town to walk about. There is a Great Barn and a ruined Abbey on the outskirts as well. I teetered to bed that night under the gaze of David Jason, who must have also found this a good place to stay, leaving his signed photograph and best wishes behind. I spent the following day, Sunday, circling the Colne Valley, But for York, I might still be there now. Bures, Wormingford, Little Horkesley, West Bergholt, Boxted, Nayland... One arm of the Constable family came from these parts. It is an endless network of lanes – not easily retraceable. I stopped to study White Colne church, picked out behind an oak in a burst of sun. Then, picking up Titanium, I found I had a puncture. Miles from anywhere.

'There's a chap at the bungalow – he'll help you out' said a man I met walking his dog. 'A hundred yards down the road.'

'Thanks!'

'You'll see him in the garden…' His voice trailed away, and I trailed on.

John Halls – a Wallace and Grommit character in a blue smock and cut-down Wellingtons – was forking up some kind of brassica from his vast vegetable plot, a hundred yards from the house.

'Just seeing to my dinner', he said. (It was only half-past ten.)

'I'll be with you in a minute.' He – like all godsends – seemed to be expecting me.

'Now what's the trouble?'

'A gentleman up the road said you might be able to help me.'

'Yes, Joe. Out with the dog.'

'I've got a puncture.'

'Well, we'll soon see to that.'

Between searches for levers and excursions to the garden and the kitchen, he fixed the bike. It wasn't easy. My puncture outfit was too old to be of any use.

'I've gor some of those new self-adhesive patches, somewhere', he said. I hadn't even got a pump.

'I've got a compressor', he said and bustled about in the dark interior of a Nissen hut, half the size of an aircraft hangar. John had everything. By the time he had finished, he had replaced the valve as well as mended the puncture – but we failed to find any thorn.

'A flint, maybe', he surmised.

I asked him if I could give him anything.

'My mother always said if you can't help somebody it's too bad', he replied. 'Where are you going?'

He gave me precise directions for getting to Wormingford, with the patience of Job, and went back to preparing his dinner. I arrived at Matins at Wormingford church, only a quarter of an hour late.

Word from Wormingford had reached me at Christmas in the shape of a book by a much-loved author, Ronald Blythe. I had written to him and told him I was planning to make this trip. I was to call at Bottengoms Farm, John Nash's old home, where Ronald now lived. Spring being in the air, however there was a certain mischief in my mind. I would surprise Ronald at the church, where he is the lay reader. With my new-found buoyancy, I bowled along. The whole valley was a jubilate. There were primroses in every ditch, magnolias illuminating every Court and Grange, drifts of daffodils in every drive, fountains of forsythia – all switched on for Mothers' Day. (Mothering Sunday, I should say.)

There was Ronald, a small figure, nimbus white hair on a prophet's head, with the rest of him engulfed in cassock, surplice and ambient apricot hood. In his address, he spoke movingly about our three kinds of mother: our own parent, Mary Mother of Jesus, and Mother Earth. He spoke as sparely as he writes, turning a nice phrase, but not drawing too much attention to it. I revelled in his references to Kilvert who wrote so movingly about primroses and children. The whole service was happy and familial. We exchanged greetings afterwards – we, and many of the other people there. I was to go to tea at Bottengoms Farm at three o'clock.

The jewelled churches of the Colne Valley in their crisp setting occupied me all the early afternoon. There were signs that villagers were beginning to leave their winter hibernations to set their gardens: a fresh-tilled patch of earth, a fork left in the ground... I was ready for tea with Ronald Blythe, there in his scallop-shell of quiet, down an unmade track, surrounded by a garden quite impossible to fathom. In John Nash's old farmhouse, he leads a preserved way of life. Paintings and books inhabit the house, it seems, more than he does. He is their keeper. But he is eminently practical; and his tea and cake were as good as conversation. Insights are what he offers: a fragile vision of a community of people in tune with their surroundings, with one another – and so with themselves. It is a special kind of beatitude.

Thrice blessed, I cycled on to Dedham and its famous church where I missed only the first quarter of Evensong, arriving in time for the Nunc Dimittis. Later I repaired to the Marlborough Head where I toasted myself with a half of bitter and a hot cheese sandwich by a roaring fire, skimmed through the Daily Mirror and fell into conversation with an ambulance man. He did not say 'Poor devil', or 'rather you than me', when I told him I was cycling to York. He thought I looked fit for my age.

'Dare I arsk, 'ow old you arh?'

'Seventy-two'. I lied.

'Blowdy 'ell!'

'I've had a few hiccups along the way', I confessed. 'Spondylitis, for instance.'

'Ow theyat's owld oige', he said, crossing his legs with fervour at the thought of me being carried into coronary care. 'Yow're allowud theyat!'.

He agreed with me that the papers were full of rubbish. He'd been sailing all day. Meeting his girl friend later.

'Carry on, moite!', he called as I left, and he sprawled nearer the fire.

I walked back to my digs at the Rookery – an old farm whose land had been gobbled up by the new A12 – under the same stars that Constable knew: Orion, Cassiopeia, the Plough… An owl hooted next morning at five, as my landlandy said it would do. I was dressed, breakfasted and ready for off at eight. I crossed the Suffolk border about nine and descended on Flatford Mill.

There is nothing left of the bustling industrial workplace that Constable knew. This whole valley and beyond – as far as Ipswich – saw the eruption of the iron industry which sparked off the industrial revolution, which enabled agriculture to advance with the aid of machines, which brought prosperity to the miller and the boat-yard in turn. There is no flavour of that now. It is as dead as Coalbrookdale. Tired of more churches – East Bergholt and Long Melford – Titanium tossed me off at Sudbury, where I needed a change of film. Gainsborough commands the town from his plinth, easel and brush in hand. I could not but admire his legs – stout as those of Clive in the market square at Shrewsbury. I wished I had his legs… Safe in my chalet, however, at something after midnight, I counted my money – and my blessings. LUCKY TO BE ALIVE, I wrote in my diary. DOWN TO FORTY POUNDS.

The girl who served breakfast in the morning also took the money.

'Forty-eight pounds', she said.

'I haven't got it', said I.

'Oh, alright, thirty-eight.'

'And the bike?'

'The laundryman will get it for you now.'

The laundryman directed me out of town. 'Thetford, straight up. Roman road.'

There, at half past eleven, I found Tom Paine, coat-tails flying, on his statue in the middle of the town.

>JUSTICE IS DUE TO EVERYMAN:
>I SEEK NO RECOMPENSE –
>I FEAR NO CONSEQUENCES…

Proud words. He looked like a wicked dancing master, giving England the slip, already on his way to America.

I was rebuked in the museum for not shedding my ruck-sack at the door.

'More than my life is worth', I quipped. 'I've already been round.'

There were Balderstons at Thetford, as there were at Little Ness. I walked round the Priory with Titanium while groundsmen played catch-me-up with their mowers and CBs. Soon, I was on my way to Kings Lynn.

Kings Lynn has all the faded grandeur of Rochester, but none of its atmosphere. It lacks elevation – an irremediable defect. Miserable little coal-black, puce and yellow terrace houses on the edge of the town sport names like Deganwy, Delhi and The Riviera. One was simply called Locum. The boarding houses were cheap: thirteen pounds for one person, twelve for two, eleven for three… I wondered what was going on. No one answered the door. A notice offered a phone number to ring. Why would anyone do that? At about the fourth door, I heard a shuffling and, presently, a breaking of the seals. A lady, the size and colour of a Charlolais cow, looked down at me. I remembered all those French landladies and their looks when I asked 'Avez vous une chambre Madame?' She left me in a dark passage while she sought information from the back of the house. I studied the grease on the walls – a mixture of medieval emulsion, condensation and smoke, no doubt – and hoped the answer would be no.

'Vell, darling, iss like this', said a shorter woman, emerging from the back. 'Za power workers are in, an' za rooms are full. Zer iz vun viv vun a'ready in viv room vor two.'

She was like someone out of Crime and Punishment, raddled but surviving, toothless but done up like an old music-hall star. Cosmopolitan as those old terrace houses. Defiant against time and change.

'No thanks', I said. 'I'm too old for that.'

I thought I should have to sleep in a dyke that night, but eventually found something. Angel House at Watlington, a few miles west of Kings Lynn, was really SOMETHING. Whole counties of England coyly keep quiet about their B&Bs. You have to go to Herefordshire to see signs of a woman's willingness to sell eggs as well as her cooking and laundry skills. All over Worcestershire, men set out garden produce by the roadside, trustingly. Honey - usually the man's preserve - is advertised FOR SALE. Neighbouring Shropshire is not so flush with her wares. The Forest of Dean is excellent. The West Country folk hang over their gates to pull you in. Berkshire is too posh; Buckinghamshire too prim; Hampshire too self-possessed; Kent too prone to invasion anyway; and Middlesex is Middlesex, overshadowed by London, which is impossible.

Imagine my delight, then, when heading into Lincolnshire – which has not many gates for people to hang over – I came across Angel House. Who, having a property with a name like that, would not advertise it? Who would not set it about with wrought iron gates? Who would not have a boy at hand to call the traveller in?

'Wait there', he said, leaving me just inside the front door of the house, 'I'll go and see.'

Presently a strong, blonde young woman came to ask what I wanted.

'A room for the night.'

'Single? £29.'

Done!

Boy, dark and handsome, shouldered my bags and led me out to the chalets. Blonde followed with key and instructions about breakfast and Sam. Sam was a collie, more handsome than they. He fixed on me and, when I went into my room, lay by my bike outside. He was my minder.

'Don't mind Sam', said the brisk young blonde. 'He'll go in the house for the night.' With that, she and the dark young man departed. They seemed to have finished for the day. I was the last, if not the only, chick to be shut up for the night. Sam lay patiently, low to the ground, outside my pen. I devoured coffee and biscuits by the half-open French window. He showed no interest, except in guarding my bike. Then the girl came back and said I could put my bike under cover for the night up at the house. She showed me to a kind of basement shed. I put the chain and lock on it. Sam still stayed there, guarding it – for all I know – all night.

I breakfasted at the house next morning, idly enquiring of the host and hostess, the relationships of the characters I had met last night.

'Sam's ours', they said. 'He lives in.'

'Is the boy the girl's brother?'

'She wouldn't thank you for that!'

I shut up and got on with my meal.

Soon I was heading for Boston; but all the signs wanted to take me to Wisbech, Spalding or Sleaford – a place I had never heard of. I passed through battlefields of daffodils, all drilled to perfection. I saw a few rangy Longhorns that looked badly in need of improvement by Coke. After Suffolk, I saw no sheep. All arable, as we say in Shropshire, where you can still be held up by chickens crossing the road. In soggy Lincolnshire the only crowing you hear is of container lorries, like fiery dragons, panting uphill and plunging down. If is, of course, mostly down to the ports. Coned off sections of these fast roads mean that the rag-tag-and-bobtail are pushed to the side. There a thin safety zone marked by a white line narrows alarmingly. You may be left lying like Ophelia in a flower-strewn dyke. I composed an anthem to the White-liners, the White-Ribboners, as we called the Band of Hope, the back-bone of the temperance movement which was still active in my youth. It contained phrases like 'safe in the arms of Jesus' and 'where is my poor wandering boy tonight', but the tune was lost in the tumult.

Occasionally Titanium and I fell upon a grassy bank, the western (hidden) side of which was colonised by cowslips or violets. There were mattresses of celandines in the drier dykes. Occasionally a stray daffodil trumpeted on its own, keeping a gypsy's distance from the conforming crowd. Nature is endlessly entertaining when it is wilful and wild.

Such breathing spaces, however, were rare. Finally, at Fosdyke we hit traffic lights as well as cones. Impatient diesels body-checking one another, took me for a fly-half and bundled me into touch. I hit the dirt. One driver slowed, as if to sympathise. The hooting and crowing went on. I was aware that I had a pound of black Lincoln loam somewhere over my left eye, but felt no blood. Titanium was unconcerned. We trundled on. The lights were holding the traffic behind, allowing us to settle again. Head down to Boston, boy! Who shall we find to comfort us there?

'Thank God for the Stump!' I wrote on my card which I sent home from Boston that night. 'You see it for miles from the north.' (I must have meant south!) 'Tail wind and slipstreams of lorries helped. Wet! Found lovely B&B near the church, which I must now go and see. Also second-hand books. So guess what I got? Kinglake's travels. (Harder than mine!) Lincoln next. Then Brigg. Then York.'

The famous church was locked at 4.30 p.m. 'For evensong', said an official whom I encountered hurrying away about an hour later. He might have been the organist. He wore gloves, a mack and trilby, and carried a briefcase. He had an air of wishing to depart in peace, and not be asked awkward questions by a casual visitor. I fell into conversation with a policeman, who had time on his hands. Together, we studied the mysterious movements of a swarm of jackdaws and pigeons flying in and out of the Stump. It is one of those English landmarks like Nelson's Column, conveniently measured at 365 ft. We concluded that the pigeons were unsettling the jackdaws, or vice-versa. 'Big as it is, there's not room for all that lot', he said and plodded on. After I looked around the town, the old wharves and warehouses, neither pigeons or jackdaws were about. The Stump boomed seven, and I stumped off to my digs.

Thanks mainly to Kinglake, I failed to get to know my landlady till morning. She had told me on arrival that she was new to the job, didn't know whether she had done right, liked to go to bed early and assured me that I could have breakfast at seven. Farmhouse. ''Ave a goood showwa. Eet's a reelly lovely showwa!' It was.

Kinglake kept me awake with his first encounter with the Bedouin. *'As I advanced, some twenty or thirty of the most uncouth-looking fellows imaginable came forward to meet me… They were tall, powerful fellows, but repulsively ugly… I advanced to a gap in the fence, and at one alighted from my horse… Presently I found myself seated upon a sheepskin spread for me under the sacred shade of Arabian canvas.'*

It was as simple as that. But, when I thought about it, I considered myself just as fortunate to be welcomed into the house of a very pretty lady who did not know me from Adam, yet had set at my disposal a room, a bed, writing table, easy chairs – and those indispensable facilities, an electric kettle and sachets of tea, coffee, sugar, and tublets of milk. Her father, she told me at breakfast, had been a farmer and remembered delivering milk with a horse and cart in the town. She herself had only recently left that way of life. She had two dogs – both strays – which she armed and lapped and cosseted all the time. They were like her children.

'They down't mowlt ya see, they're now trewble at aw – they're lovely!' In addition to the two dogs – small and nearly as pretty as her – there were two cats, kept in different regions of the house. Her last guests were Taiwanese. 'Couldn't speak of word of English, but we got on lovely.' She was looking forward to the summer when she could fill her home with visitors. 'Oi shawn't ever be lowmly, ya see.'

At half past seven I was ready to leaves.

'Thank you Mrs – er -.'

'Meece – oi'm Meece, reelly. They got me down in the fown book as Mrs, but oi never married. Oi s'pows it's best to be Mrs…' And she was so pretty. Reader, I could have married her.

From Boston to York I let my diary lapse. Churches preoccupied my thoughts. Titanium must have been chained to more church railings than any other bike on earth. No wonder he eventually rebelled. But, for the time being, all was straightforward. The wind from the south blew us into Boston, then blew us into Brigg. Lincoln was a hilly hiccup in between.

You see more of the cathedral from the southern approaches of the city than you do from the high street, named Steep Hill. All that talk about the Seven Wonders of the World – and there in Lincoln is the biggest of them all! How did our short ancestors – short of stature and short of machinery – get it all up there? (They were, of course, not so short of faith, skill or time.) I yoked Titanium to a bollard half way up the hill named Steep, and struggled on. My first thought on entering the cathedral was: where are the toilets, where is the tea? The unastonished lady on the door pointed me in a distant easterly direction. SEATING REMOVED TO ENHANCE THE VISITOR'S VIEW OF THE BUILDING. It was exactly as I imagined Jonah's view of the inside of the whale, when I was a child. St Hugh's Choir and the Angel Choir made up for it – and the stained glass, all rhododendron reds and blues.

In the coffee shop, I noticed a dark-suited gentleman in earnest conversation with a waitress at a table nearby. No simple-minded tourist he. After visiting the toilet a second time, I realised I had left my rucksack behind at the coffee shop.

'John's got it – he's looking for you in the cathedral', said the waitress. Before I could get back to the nave, however, I spotted John in his office. 'I knew you'd be back', he smiled. I thanked him for his help and slipped in a cheeky question.

'Have you got rid of your deans?'

'One of them', he smiled. 'We keep our heads above water. It's places that matter, not people, you know.'

We had found a real bond in my rucksack.

It was as straight as a Roman road could be to Brigg. The wind blew. I blew. Titanium didn't blow, yet – but for days now I had noticed a slight swelling in the back tyre, a slight exposure of the inner tube between the outer and the rim. It was like a rupture of the intestine, rudimentary, perhaps, but work keeping under observation, as they say…

'It's places that matter, not people, you know.' I was to debate John's dictum for the rest of my tour. 'Places matter more than people, in the end', is probably what he said. Not that people don't matter at all. Places, people and <u>things</u>. I was beginning to have very strong feelings for Titanium. He was so tolerant. Whatever the time of day, whatever the weather, he was ready to go. No fuel injection needed; no injection, even, of air. Just gentle persuasion, and a pat now and again.

We held on to Hibaldstow, just outside Brigg, where my old school friend Geoff has a guest house. He reminded me that we had not met for 56 years.

He showed me my room and installed Titanium in a shed. Geoff has been a professional cyclist – as well as Fleet Air Arm mechanic, policeman, hotelier and a few other things – so he has a due sense of priorities.

'Will a steak at the pub be alright tonight? I don't cook, myself. Only breakfasts.'

A steak at the pub seemed alright to me.

'I phoned Eddie as soon as I knew you were arriving', Geoff said. 'I told him we've got our man. He's coming to join us at the pub.'

Eddie is another school friend – even more ancient than Geoff. So now we were ready for reminiscence: three men at a pub. Plus one – the publican, himself.

Sad, but I hardly saw Brigg. Cobbett described it as a delightfully pretty place. Used to skinning my eyes to keep Titanium on the road in the dark, rubbing them with my fingers to make starlight, it was strange to be boxed in a car and whisked to The White Horse without needing to move a muscle. All my motor movements, all decisions removed from my hands. I just did as I was told. And revelled in the telling.

'The church is not just the building; neither is the school', our old Little Ness teacher used to tell us – annoyed that we could not see ourselves as a brotherhood. Ah, but we did not then know about the pub! Beams, pewter tankards and coziness do not make a pub; but two hundred years of practice helps. Cobbett may not have known The White Horse. Evidently it used to be a farm on the outskirts of Brigg amid orchards and barley fields. It had only one storey, the water-table being so high. What is now the lounge used to be the cellar. It was transmogrified in 1927 – the year I was born. I like to think of something as perfect as The White Horse and something as imperfect as me receiving our more or less definitive form at the same time. And coming together, albeit many years later, by chance – and in the dark. Geoff, Eddie and I: the Three Malteers. And there was Tom Merriman, our host at the bar.

'What will you have?'

'Oh, just half a bitter, please.' (The others' choices were more exotic than mine. I stick with Cobbett – and the men whose tankards, individually owned, still hung over the bar, though I could not match their girth.) Tom might have played D'Artagnan in his youth, but he has exchanged his cloak for a butcher's apron and lost his hat and his hair. He is, though, still quick on the draw. The White Horse is better than a drama school – and better by far than cookery on TV.

Leaving the enlightenment of the bar, we retired to our table in the lounge for our meal. I am afraid I am one of those old-fashioned people who like their food well-cooked, so mine was the well-done steak. What better praise is there in life than 'Well done!?' After subsisting for a week mainly on apples and Mars Bars, I was in danger of being bowled over. I was. Tom's wife bore in three heaped platters, prettily beaming with pride. Prettily beamed the steak, couched in its bed of chips and vegetables under a cover of sauce. The latter had an aroma of wine, onions and mushrooms, and, perhaps, a vintage stock. 'Tom does the cooking', she said. Later, Tom – with a goblet of Burgundy – came to relax at our table and collect our thanks. 'I like to be sociable on the job', he said. And it was evident that he was the same with everybody – but a little more so with us. Initially. I had more in common with Geoff and Eddie; they had been to school with me.

'Tell your brother I've forgiven him for punching me on the lip and making it bleed', Geoff said.

Eddie, slightly older, remembered John better than me. Through correspondence, however, I was able to flesh out the rather Pickwickian figure that sat beside me now. He was a master grocer and a mason in the town. A pillar of society. He and Geoff had travelled the world as conscripts after the war; their talk was sprinkled with allusions to the Gulf of Mexico, Sydney and Durban – where Geoff certainly admitted to swanning around 'for about six months.'

'So, what did John do?'

'Oh, he was in radar at TRE, Malvern.' (No orthodox avenues for John.) Geoff had been in the police, engineering and the hotel trade. He was an ace cyclist. Was there anything he had not done? I kept quiet about my piecemeal career. (If you tell people you have been a teacher, that is enough.)

I was drawn towards the end of the meal to Tom, sitting there, proprietorially proud in his apron, waving his goblet of Burgundy in the warm night air. Waving is the wrong word: it moved in his hand in a gentle ellipse, a caressing, rotary oscillation, like rocking a favourite child to sleep. In fact, I don't think he drank much of the wine. It remained, dipping and rising, playing in the low light, lambent and precious – too precious to put down. A smile played on the face of our host. He knew a good thing.

'I put out the red carpet for all my customers', he said.

It only served to make me feel more special. I wanted to know all about this connoisseur, as mesmeric and well-preserved as his drink. Eddie and Geoff excused themselves – I thought to go to the loo. Tom talked on. Burgundy travelled round and round that glass.

'I think they're waiting for you', Tom said. (Cycling, I never have a watch.)

'Sorry – thanks!' I stumbled out, still not knowing what time of day – or night – it was.

Back at Hibaldstow, I wrote in my diary: YOU CAN STILL SEE THE BEST OF ENGLAND AT A PUB – IF YOU FIND THE BEST PUB. I lay on my bed thinking how strange life was. When you are young there is an infinity of possibilities open to you, but chance and circumstance throw spanners in the works. Three of us old Shrewsbury boys had started out more or less on the same track, diverged for nearly sixty years, then came together again at a signal, like trains, then clockworked off again. I should see Geoff in the morning – but only for about an hour. Their course in life had been totally different from mine. They had done orderly, orthodox things. They had not had more, nor less, chances than I. They had simply taken different ones. We had all travelled; but I, it seemed, had wandered more than they. I had lived more like a gypsy, subsisting close to the ground; they had settled to a plummier line of life.

The burgundy travelled round and round the glass…

NOBODY NEED ENVY ANYONE ELSE, I wrote, then wondered if Eddie had had any Mrs Bardells in his life. My life - like John's – had followed a very flat curve. No very high peaks; no very low troughs. A kind of level subsistence, all the way. I was reminded of this when getting money – for the first time in my life – from a hole in the wall. It was in Thetford. I had to wrestle to remember my pin-number.

Lying on my bed, I looked round at Geoff's superbly appointed accommodation. I suddenly remembered March 1950 when John, my brother, and I arrived at a sunny Amalfi. We had hitch-hiked down from Milan, been caught up in a religious procession in Perugia – nuns chanting 'Ora pro nobis' through the cobbled streets – been blessed by the Pope on Easter Day in Rome, then escaped murder in the backstreets of Naples and arrived in sun-drenched Amalfi. I jotted it down for Geoff to see in the morning. (People always want to know what you are carrying off in your diary.)

Narrow ledges of road, ending in white-walled town. Evening. Tanned youths loitering. Hungry, tired, we looked for a place for the night. Followed a youth through tunnels, deep, mysterious. Emerged at la signora's…

La signora, a crone, a cackling witch, bent, crabbed, gap-toothed, shawled…
led us upstairs to small room with bare electric light bulb, pointed like a spear,
which sprang out of a crack in the wall from an s-bend pipe that carried the
flex. A sword of Damocles. Landlady left us, cackling down creaking stairs.
Room smelt of coconut matting left damp and unaired. John slept with pocket
knife open under pillow. Opened window first in case… There was stale bread
and sour cheese in the morning.

We lived on bread and cheese on that trip – and Chianti. TANTO
FORMAGGIO E TANTI CHIESI! I remembered seeing goat's cheese
hanging in skins like bulls' testicles in dark market places – but we could
afford only the crumbs off the counters, thank God.

Geoff set a marvellous breakfast for me, meaning to get me off to a good,
early start. How could I have imagined he would wish to hear about i poveri
in Italian.

Two miles out of Brigg, I wrote on my postcard home

My back tyre went. Turned into cycle factory just over the bridge. Former
cycling champion, George Lea greeted me at the gate. 'I'll see you right', he
said. A young man just arriving for work took the wheel out and brought it
back less than five minutes later with new tyre. That's how lucky I am!

'You must go through Beverley', said Geoff; and very glad I was that I
did. I had the second-best fish and chips of my tour at the Bee Hive – the
ultimate best being at Tate's in Boston. About the sickliest-looking man I
have ever seen came in and declared that he never ate fish out. Perhaps he
should have done.

People promenade round Beverley in the free and easy way they do in all
Minster towns – especially in the afternoon. As the Portuguese, Italians,
Greeks, Turks and others lucky enough to live nearer the tropics promenade
later, in the cool of the evening. It is as much to do with light as it is to do
with warmth, though; and, on this beautiful March day, you could be forgiven for thinking you were in Corfu or that it was early summer, not
spring. I photographed the Minster towers, a paean of limestone, duetting
heavenwards to the accompaniment of a silver birch. The tree in the foreground matched their airy lightness, enhanced by the fresh blue of the sky
– such as you seldom see later in the year. A horse-chestnut with a few fin-
ger-like fronds confirmed that it was spring. Docile Titanium stood by the

railings, unchained. It would not be long till he was.

Inside, the Minster seemed spring-cleaned. If this is Gothic, I thought, let me have more. But this is the ultimate. No heavy entablature, no dark-stained glass, no pomp and circumstance. Tombs, if there were any, had shrunk to their proper perspective. You have to hunt for the misericords. The whole is a stylistic unity, surprising because it has had to be rebuilt several times. The woodwork is as aspiring as the stonework. Uplifting, as all places of worship should be. Why is it closed at 4 p.m?

I had to get to York. 'Don't baulk – go to York!' I chanted to myself. I thought of W H Auden's marvellous poem 'In Praise of Limestone', of which I cannot remember a line – only the essence. Which is what I mean to remember of Beverley – and all the great things I have seen.

About four hours later, I bowled into York. WELCOME TO THE CITY OF YORK, said the sign about four flat miles out. I had a map, gripped in my cold right hand. The first car headlights came on. I must not, could not, be beaten now. This A1079 went on for ever. A few factory-like buildings began to occupy the limitless space that is the Vale of York. Roadsides without gates, habitations, gardens – not to mention animal and human life – are alien to me. I was drained by the exhaustingly unvaried monoculture of the Fens. I had to think back to those banks of cowslips and violets which had successfully turned their faces away, the clock back, defying Man's tinkering with their world.

For me, however, time and change hurried on. Garages sprung electrified up. Private cars appeared out of drives, with people obviously dressed for a night on the town; the theatre perhaps. And the traffic was going all one way. My way. At last I came to Walmgate Bar. So pleased was I to enter the celestial city I quite forgot the Tourist Centre's instructions to follow the A1079 outside the city wall to Bootham where I would find my B & B. A lady pedestrian put me right. Darkness, and the increased traffic circling the city, drove me to the safety of the pavement, here and there marked as a cycle track. Foss Islands Road...St Maurice's Road...Lord Mayor's Walk...Turn left into Gillygate...Then right... I rehearsed my route, still gripping my crumpled map. It was really dark now. Walk a bit. Ride a bit... 'I thought only school children did that', shouted a huge man who was walking his dog towards me.

'Oh, shut up!', I replied, then walked on.

Presently, however, I felt his hand grip my arm. His demonic face appeared uncomfortably close to mine.

'You swore at me', he fumed.

'I told you to shut up', I affirmed as calmly as I could.

He was Mephistophelean. Lank black hair hung about smouldering eyes. 'You swore', he mouthed repeatedly, bearing down on me, his flesh white with Old Testament rage. Was he possessed?

'You leave that man alone', said a lady, also walking her dog. And he complied without demur. Did she know him, I wondered? Had he done this to cyclists before? It left me shaken, as I dutifully padded along Lord Mayor's Walk.

The next day , I sat in York Minster and thanked God for my deliverance. The words were all there in my head, remembered from of old. You only had to rehearse them: *from all perils and dangers of this night…who hast safely brought us to the beginning of this day…* ' I pity the poor traveller who does not have these words in his heart. And, like R S Thomas, I am nothing religious… You think of hobgoblins and foul fiends, of Apollyon and men going about as wolves, seeking whom they may devour… Our modern secular words and phrases like 'container lorry', 'road rage' or 'juggernaut' seem like Dinky toys. The word that comes to mind as you sit by God's hearth in York is 'dwelling-place'. There is an amplitude of chairs here. You are under no compulsion to move, you can stay as long as you like. God provided the space; and Man the ample furnishings. And what furnishings!

Poking around among the tombs, you see a great bishop or archbishop of the seventeenth century sprawling idly like a lover – three cherubs floating over him.

'He looks too lazy to get off his back', said a lady guide, 'yet he fought at Marston Moor'.

Sad memorials of soldiers from the York and Lancaster regiment who fell in the Indian Mutiny line the South Transept wall. 'Erected by their comrades..' Archbishop Thompson lies in full view at the end of the nave with his dog at his feet. 'Rascal' says my lady guide.

Half the towers outside are under scaffolding or wrapped in a bandage of polythene, but inside all seems well. You can scarcely believe that even God could keep his house in such good order, especially after the recent fire… You try to take in everything – the great west window, the roof bosses, the fan vaulting, the wood carving of the choir – but you are lost. Majesty does not come as a flat-pack; it cannot be assembled piece by piece.

'Fairfax saved York', you hear the lady guide tell another astonished set of ears and eyes. But that was in 1644, three and a half centuries after building was begun. Three and a half centuries later, work still goes on. Evensong at 4 p.m. brings all this into balance. Wilbye (1574 – 1638) set the canticles; Buxtehude (1637 – 1707) composed the anthem; and the Fairfax Singers from Leeds took the part of the choir (on holiday before Easter). How's that for continuity?

My landlady at Canterbury thought I was marvellous, and told her husband so. My landlady at York was less impressed – I had broken a saucer in my room in a vain attempt to wash up, and she appeared to have no husband to tell. Besides, I had arrived in York on a bicycle; to Canterbury I had walked – the whole of the Pilgrims Way. 'It happens', said my landlady in York, with a sigh – seeming to add 'but not very often'. To her, I was no phenomenon – just another of the rag-tag and bobtail of tourism, walkers and cyclists who cannot afford to stay at hotels. Here today and gone tomorrow, we are invited to give details of our identity at the desk; but having no car and no family in attendance, we are – let's face it – not likely to return. We are one-offs, only likely to stay one night or, at the most, two. We are as the dust under the bed, the empty sachets of coffee and sugar in the bin under the sink along with the milk tubs and teabags – and those brittle hemispheres of pottery about which there was nothing to be done. And nothing was.

But there is another side to the coin – the saucer, if you like. These English landladies, so like one another in some respects, so private and so apparently unconcerned, are themselves unique. Their service is almost perfect freedom. Once you have registered at the desk and they given you the key to your room, you are free to bathe, shower, loll on your bed, watch television, brew up, listen to the blackbird singing in the garden outside, stay in, go out, and come back when you please. (A simple security device on the outside door seems only to add to your sense of proprietorship, not tenancy.) 'Breakfast is from half past seven till nine', you are roundly informed. 'Full English?' 'The works, please', you reply, if you are a rag-tag and bobtail tourist like me. 'You need a good start to the day.' English landladies all believe in good sound sleep and a good breakfast. A notice in the room tells you that you are expected to be out of it by ten in the morning – well that's fair enough. There are those two hemispheres of clay to be removed. You feel less guilty about the state of the bed because you have decided to stay two nights; and you may leave your bags in the room – on that score, there is never a worry. You feel just as carefree as the blackbird, singing out there in the garden again. What goes on behind those gravy-brown doors marked PRIVATE is no concern of yours. Somehow, between the hours of your departure in the morning and return in the evening, all that washing-up, cleaning and bed-making has been done. You have floated airily as a balloon round places of interest while the hoover has picked up your dirt.

Somehow, you imagine – as you admire Man's Masonic masterpieces, his cathedrals, his museums and art galleries – that England is held together by landladies. Man parades his memorials, literally: the effigies and monumental statues to men far outnumber those to women. (I can think of only two in London: Edith Cavell and Boadicea.) Think, however, what the world would be like if landladies came from behind their closed doors and set about the rest of us. They would be a far more formidable force than the Women's Institute or the Mothers' Union. It is as well for us walkers and cyclists that they don't! So, there may never be an anthem for these, the unsung heroines of our race. Their influence is, however, detectable abroad, especially in New Zealand where 'the great English breakfast' still stands the farming communities and the tourists in good stead. Maybe, the gold-diggers there and in the Yukon were fortified by it, too. Certainly our EU partners have missed out in this respect.

Imagine the relief with which early travellers, seeking whatever fortune in the longer term, came upon a lodging house in some pioneer community at the end of a long, foot-slogging day. Some daughter or grand-daughter from a well black-leaded English farm kitchen would be there – among other, more elusive ladies – to meet their basic needs. It makes you realise that not only England but the Empire was held to-gether by landladies. They were there. Before the men even got there, they had somehow set up house and called it home. So, you pitch into York, or Canterbury, Winchester or Yarmouth, Hereford or Glastonbury, and you find a land-lady there. It may be late in the day, your hopes fading with the light; you may think you have come to the end of the world and the end of your life, your strength ebbing as your heart sinks with the sun that set you free in the morning with the illusion of limitless energy and time. Ecce mulier! She is there! Notices saying NO VACANCIES become childhood fears, now that you hear her say yes, she has a single, not en suite, but near the bathroom – and you can leave your bike at the back... No one will touch it there. It is a world away from the disobliging old crone in Paris who scrawled on my Youth Hostel card: 'Not welcome to return'. (I had only requested an unusually early departure time.) Then there was the Black Widow of Amalfi, about whom I must not tell you again…

Suddenly, one realises that the English landlady is a metaphor for England itself. Suddenly, too, one realises the full, painful significance of that sentence of Jacquetta Hawkes: *'Even the stern white front that Albion turns to the Continent is withdrawing at the rate of fifteen inches a year.'* (It may be more like fifteen metres now.) You realise, too, that Albion is not just a lady; she may even be a nun – a saint, perhaps.

My brother, who lives in Huddersfield, collected me from York the next morning. It was Sunday. The Minster bells drowned out the service at neighbouring St Michael-in-the-Belfry. 'With difficulty', said an attendant when I asked him how they managed. He was sunning himself outside the door. 'We turn the PA system down between peals – but not for long!' It would be easy for John to find me at the station without being caught up in the inner-city throng. Stripped of his wheels, Titanium had but a tiny frame and would easily fit into the boot of his car. Barclay Card to the fore, I booked our passage from Huddersfield next day by train. It had all been so easy. I had felt the hand of providence on us all the way. Seeing Titanium dismembered on the pavement gave me mixed feelings of sadness and joy. I was reminded of my own out-of-body sensations when, the south wind to my back, I sped down to the Vale of York. The skylark that helped us uphill out of Beverley. A group of coltsfoot, like pale children, sometimes smiled as we passed. Never seen anything like it! Titanium and I, spinning along, both light of frame. Sometimes I would let out a shout that would frighten a horse, had there been any about. (Sadly, we saw only two ragged Shires by a windmill in Norfolk – and NO SUFFOLK PUNCHES!) Alternatively, I would sing shattered fragments of the more stained-glass hymns: *'Eternal ruler of the ceaseless round…Lead me all my journey through…'*

Sometimes I had the curious sensation of being simultaneously in the high farming eras of this and the last century. Prosperity was evident everywhere. If there were no vegetables in the fields, there were parsnips, cabbages and kings all over the road. North of the Wash, you felt you were in a different country. Independent. Shucks – yaboo to Westminster! But not any more. We were heading south, captive and unarmed.

Our journey by train to Reading and home was not uneventful, though. I had failed to reassemble Titanium correctly. Wheels were in place, but not chain. How did the man at the cycle factory in Brigg get the chain over the cogs? We would have to sort it out later. From Huddersfield to Manchester, Titanium was placed in a cubby-hole by the door of the compartment; a mere item of baggage. I had had to lift him onto the platform and into the train – he having his rear wheel fixed. Even more awkward was the flight of steps at Manchester, leading to the Birmingham train. There on the platform, however – with the timing of an angel – was Kevin. He was the train manager, and had a badge of office, a helpful hand and a friendly, friendly smile.

'Perhaps you have an able young man on your staff', I said 'who would help me with my bike? The chain's not properly on.'

Somewhere between Stockport and Birmingham, Kevin, our train manager, wished all passengers a pleasant journey over the PA, adding that he would shortly be walking through the train. We were to let him know if we had any queries. Presently Kevin appeared, accompanied by a young, equally smiling, attendant.
'You may thank him', he said 'he nicked it oop in the guard's van.'
And there, but for twenty-five hard miles home from Reading, this part of the story ends. Sadly for Titanium, his owner did not seem to share my pride in him and he was stolen one dark winter night.

An inquisitive Northumbrian pig cocks a snout at me!

Au revoir Titanium! En avant, Elan – my second-hand Raleigh greyhound who cost only twenty pounds and weighed about the same. I went ostensibly to dally round the Dales. But I could not go north again without at least seeing Durham. It was my Ultima Thule, the last resting place of Bede and St Cuthbert, the end of the spiritual rainbow. To 'do' Durham, I would need to stay there at least two days. Emerging from the station, as upon the Heights of Abraham, I had a surprisingly early, open view of the sandstone mass of the castle and cathedral. I eagerly snapped it, straight away, as if afraid that it might disappear. I worked my way round to the Market Place, where people were sitting about on public seats in the sun. Durham is a very public place. There is probably a very low crime rate in a city so open, friendly and pedestrianised. Most people seem to walk in Durham: students, tourists and the easily recognised veterans of the place. It is death to cyclists; and cars are only seen distantly, wheeling like mayflies on the shiny, river-like roads that, via Framwelgate or Milburngate, lead out of the city. Only cobbled streets lead in. Stamina and strength are written all over Durham.

The church in the Market Place offers teas. It was here that, between 1975 and 1982, George Carey was vicar. 'Ee's booke's ova theer', said George Scott who was on duty in the basement café. He told me all about 'Door'm'. I no sooner left the church than, standing gawping at the Town Hall, I fell into the arms of the Mayor. He showed me round. I admired the full-length portrait of Sir Robert Peel. 'Born in Richmond' he said. The Town Hall is mostly of 1850 construction – a symphony in stone and wood with flourishes of Victorian stained glass. It speaks of amplitude and prosperity – the high-water mark of English agriculture and industry. We discussed Peel's contribution to this through the repeal of the Corn Laws.

'Before the decline at the end of the century', I suggested.

'I've joost poot t'getha a booke', said the Mayor. 'Aw be meself. I'll giya a coppy.' He rifled through a drawer in the great oak desk in his parlour. 'I'm notta pen-poosha. I like t'sell Door'm.' I thanked him and went on my way. For all that it is only twenty loose-leaf pages, I would rather have George Young's booke than George Carey's.

I had met George Scott and George Young; now wandering down South Street, next morning, I literally fell upon Frank Lockerbey. He told me that is the correct spelling of his name. He is an ex-miner. Seventy-six. He walked this way every morning with his little dog – well, it's not his really, it's his neighbour's. It was a nice little thing, and he enjoyed the walk.

I had been photographing the castle and the cathedral – again – from the heights. I knew that eventually I might gain legitimate access to the river-side path through the ivy over-growing the embankment and tumble precipitately down. No surprise to Frank who, of course, was taking the official route. He was short and walked slowly with a stick; but his hair was Northumbrian black and his face unlined with, however, a tell-tale plumpness which was perhaps too pink.

'Ah useta do that', he volunteered, twinkling like a schoolboy. 'They shood neva a shoot that oaf', he said, pointing to the short piece of chestnut fencing at the end of the path. 'They'd no rights.'

Together we ambled almost all round the horseshoe which is the towpath which leads, by one lot of seventy steps or another, back to the market place. Frank pointed out the boat-houses, the Little Count's house – vandalised by students – and, taking his stick, created a conduit for an unwanted puddle on the muddy path to find its way back to the river.

'Ah do that iv'ree dae', he says.

Frank has lived in Door'm all his life. He worked in the mines, as did his father before him. I struggled to conceive how such a small tottery old man could ever have had the strength to do such hard work for so many long hours, days, weeks, years... We talked about the gala. This year's might be the last, he told me. The Labour politicians used to come. Soreness entered his eyes. I tried to get him to tell me more about the past, but he seemed too unreservedly proud of his city in all its spring beauty – and pleased with his present mode of life. He is one of those essentially simple and un-envious people who do good in quiet ways.

Four oarsmen in a skiff sliced through the water, skimming the surface, leaving no mark. Frank waved. 'The veterans', he said. There was no way of telling from their well-oiled, rhythmic strokes that they are not freshman from the University. Students, however, were still rubbing sleep out of their eyes. As silently, Frank ambled on his way, taking the easier path to the bridge, while I pranced up the seventy steps, losing count as I always do. I hope that the Durham Miners' Gala continues after this year, with or without the politicians. What other memorial will there be for the silent people of Durham 'who have not spoken yet'.

Enter one cathedral. No matter that it is undoubtedly the finest Norman building in Europe and has been standing here for over eight hundred years. No matter that desperate criminals, mostly murderers, banged on the bronze knocker on the broad Norman north door in the Middle Ages, seeking sanctuary – and were admitted. You tremble at the thought of them, as you trembled when you were first told about this practice as a child. You go boldly in – for the door stands open for you, and it is part of your birthright to do so.

Enter one cathedral. A shadowy figure attendant whispers and points to the 'Marks and Spencer' window behind you. He says it's supposed to represent the Last Supper. You consider that it looks like a Christmas wrapping paper collage; but there is no need to say so.

You face the gorgeous vista of the Nave. No matter that it takes £485,000 a day to maintain. You may put £2.50 in the box – but you may be coming back. You'll see.

It takes your breath away, this enormous Norman extravagance. No matter that it – and the castle alongside it – have been the home of Prince Bishops with powers equal to those of the King; that it is described in history as a Palatinate. You are welcome here.

No matter that St Cuthbert is buried here, after being dug up at Lindisfarne and carried, his body whole and uncorrupt, to some forty-seven places in Northumberland and North Yorkshire before coming here. It is most like a homecoming, coming here.

The thrill of seeing this place for the first time might possibly be compared to that of seeing one's first child. No amount of knowing what to expect can account for it. Take it for a miracle. Take it for a blessing. Take it for a sign.

Frederick Grice wrote a beautiful book 'The Bonnie Pit Laddie', which I used to read to my children. In it he describes a visit to the City by the boy and his father on a weekend shopping trip.

'They had never been inside the cathedral; they had never peeped through the gateway to the castle. All this was to them forbidden, almost alien territory, to be hurried through… Dick…always felt a thrill of pleasure as he came out of Windy Gap and saw the massive old buildings enclosing the Green… He felt an intense curiosity about those noble and ancient houses… But these were feelings that his father did not share…'

I thought of Dick as I turned my back on the Marks & Spencer window to feast my eyes on the gorgeous vista of the nave. It is so uncluttered, airy and light. Lofty and triumphant, yes, but welcoming. It would bring a smile to the face of any young or old boy; a glad light to anyone's eye. Turning right into the South Transept, I thought of both Dick and my new acquaintance, the former miner, Frank; for there is the monument to long-serving eighteenth century bishop, Shute Barrington.

'In his works of piety and munificence, he being dead yet speaketh'

Above his white marble figure, bowed in an attitude of prayer, hangs the purple banner of the Durham Miners' Union with a strange, but somehow sadly fitting, echo of those words

'THEY BEING DEAD YET SPEAKETH'

More banners, or echoes of, in the cloisters; for, wherever you go in the cathedral, you cannot escape from St Cuthbert. Videos, relics and books pertaining to... Serendipity plays its part. I could not fathom the public (free) display of his illuminated wanderings set out on the cloister walls. 'Neither can we', says Roger Norris in the Dean and Chapter Library, where I appealed to him for help. He had, however, an excellent book 'The Relics of Saint Cuthbert' in which I find treasure. It concerns the battle and victory of Neville's Cross in 1346. (Elan and I were stationed at a B & B in The Avenue, which leads to the road to Neville's Cross – the one we would be taking when we left the city the next day.)

> *'On this occasion,' I read, 'the banner (of St Cuthbert) was taken to the bat-tlefield by John Fossor, Prior of Durham (1341-74). "In the night before the battle of Durham...", writes the author..."there did appear to John Fossor, then the Prior...of Durham, a vision, commanding him to take the holy corporax cloth, which was within the corporax, wherewith St Cuthbert did cover the chal-ice when he used to say Mass, and to put the same holy relic, like unto a ban-ner cloth, upon a spear point; and on the morrow after to go and repair to a place on the West part of the city of Durham called the Redhills, and there to remain...till the end of the said battle..."'*

All this was powerful stuff, recorded in an old chronicle 'The Rites of Durham'; but what interested me was the ways our modern author, with a faint puncturing of the bombast, went on.

> *'Prior Fossor evidently thought that St Cuthbert's help in securing the victory deserved to be commemorated. Accordingly he had a new and magnificent staff made for the banner; but when the staff was made it was probably felt that a new and more sumptuous banner ought to be made to go with it; and so we learn from the Rites that: "Shortly after the battle...the Prior caused a goodly and sumptuous banner to be made...with pipes of silver, to be put on a*

staff…five yards long, with a device to take on and off the said pipes at pleasure, and to be kept in a chest in the Feretory…which banner was shewed and carried in the said abbey on festival and principal days. On the height of the (uppermost) pipe was a fair cross of silver and a wand of silver, having a fine wrought knoop of silver at either end that went athwart the banner cloth whereonto the banner cloth was fastened…and at either end of the…wand was a fine silver bell…" '

That's better than any video, so wonderfully and typically English. What, one wonders, would St Cuthbert, pledged to poverty and simplicity, have made of it all?

Before 5.30 p.m. I took my seat in the nave for Evensong. Offertory candles flickered on either side of the Neville Screen. Whether from Purbeck or Caen, all the stone pillars and archways seemed drenched in Calvados. One verger tugged at three bell ropes in turn; another, taller and more amply upholstered, glided about as if on casters, silently making all things ready, then on the cessation of a single bell, returned to usher in the main protagonists. The choir prepared to raise its silver-piped banner in music by Orlando Gibbons and William Byrd.

One of the many ponies 'talked' to on the way

Leaving Durham – God's citadel – at an ungodly hour, I was anxious to test my Raleigh Elan's ability to get to Richmond in a day. I sensed that only with my first sight of the Swale river will I know that I am really in the Dales. The Wear is a fine old waterway, but it does not have the bounce and sparkle of the Dales rivers, my brother says, that tease and delight with surprising youthfulness. Besides, I had spent two days and nights in Durham – a tenth of my allotted time. Elan was fresh. I would test him to the limit.

We bowled out of The Avenue on the south side of the town, in fog. Beside a bridge over the Wear, lay a litter of pale sandbags, like pot-belied pigs, brushed aside and left for dead by the previous week's floods. Little roadside plantations of polyanthus peered through the vaporous gloom to prove that sunshine sometimes reaches them. Eventually the A167 would lead me to Darlington, due south, but I did not want to go to Darlington. I had a choice, it seemed. At another of those perplexing roundabouts that occupy so much of England's dwindling acreage, I rejected the sign marked Darlington and took the A1(M) route south. The sun came out. The road was wide, straight and fairly traffic-free. I had the hard shoulder to myself – and Elan, who loved it. Our progress, however, was punctuated by toots of outrage, first from a car and then from two lorries. We liked lorries – they drew us along in their slipstream. Why were they so unfriendly? We were not impeding them. The wind was with us. All nature seemed to be with us; but more on our side to the left than to the right.

Presently I became aware of a colourful presence drawing us into the side and slowing us down. It had a blue flashing light. A fresh-faced policeman emerged from the passenger door.

'Are you alright?', he asked. Did he think I was drunk? So far, I believed, we had been following a perfectly straight course.

'Yes', I said, tilting back my helmet, intended to preserve me from all evil. His young, clear eyes looked into mine. He was hatless. His hair was corn yellow; his complexion pure, apart from freckles. He asked me where I was going. Didn't I know this was a motorway?

'I thought it was the A1', I replied, playing the old fool.

'The A1(M)', he elucidated, spelling it out like algebra.

'Do you want me to walk to the turn off?' there was one signed about half a mile ahead, 'or will you take my bike in the car?'

'No', he smiled, 'it might spoil the pretty paintwork. 'You ride, and we'll come along behind you.'

I had a police escort. Darlington, he assured me when we reached the turn off, was the best way to Richmond anyway. So back we were on the

A167. And very pleasing Darlington proved to be. A town full of crocuses. An old orphanage is remembered by a civic plaque. A factory chimney under scaffolding reminded one of its smoky past. The Baptist chapel on the hill out of town testified to the northerners' spirit of compassion, past and present. The Basement, what the stuffy old C of E would call the crypt, declared itself open and there were young people evidently using it. Ah, youth! Its poignancy, and high spirits! I pedalled on.

Dropping down from Durham to Richmond you begin to observe the Englishman at play. Just south of Darlington is Croft, an affluent village with a seven-arched bridge over the Tees, a Georgian Inn that spreads into a conference and sports centre where the wide street sweeps round in a curve and, tucked in before that, a most beautiful church. I, suspecting none of this, had stopped for an apple and a Mars bar by a smaller bridge to the north. The hawthorn hedges were just leafing out bright tufts of green in their perennially reassuring way. You know you are in a sunny spot when you sit by such a hedge. The parapet of the sandstone bridge was warm to the touch. A man with three Labradors came through the riverside field. 'Piper', he called after he had crossed the stile onto the road. 'Jack! Er – what's yer name?' Each dog, after sitting in the field, came through to the road. Sat. 'Aren't they good' said I. He looked at me as if I were simple. He had all the trappings of a professional trainer of gun-dogs. I had all the trappings of a tramp.

I had spotted the bend in the river ahead, and the longer multi-arched bridge; but it was only when I had rounded it on Elan that I realised that the smaller, earlier bridge spanned only a tributary of the mighty onrushing Tees. Then I spotted the church. It has a fabulous interior, which I was unable to see. I have read about it since. One of its features is a pew like several theatre boxes, which blocks the nave, raised on stilts and with a twisting stair. Under it is a tomb in a black, white and grey marble. Even more striking, however, is the 'rowdy carving' in the chancel. Tucked back in its corner of riverside glebe, the church conspires to conceal all this. It is a give-away seventeenth or eighteenth century wool church with crenellated walls, low roof and unimpressive tower. What does impress though is the loveliness of the stone. It is as if it is aware of its power to seduce. It shrinks coyly behind a small avenue of clipped yews and well-kept lawns that run down to the river. 'The church authorities reserve the right...' says a notice at the gate, warning off people like me. Ah, Croft! I could not afford to keep you in the manner to which you are accustomed. I have to leave you anyway.

Immediately after leaving Croft you know that you are in Richmondshire. Everything tells you that this is prospcrous farming country. The living is easy; and so are the roads. Soon you come to Brompton on Swale where you first catch sight of this most high-spirited of rivers. It is said that it is the fastest of our rivers; it would need to be; it is always playing catch-up with itself. At Brompton, too, you begin to feel that you are at last in the Dales. I took Elan down through a steep beech grove to the river to photograph him in celebration of his efforts in getting us here. Nothing, however, prepares you for the long hill-climb to Richmond Town. A merry speedster waved as he left town and I staggered in. I resisted St Trinians B & B at the bottom of the hill. Castle View would do. No one was in. Tried next door. No one in. Must have gone to fetch the kids from school. At 4 Pottergate I found Barbara. She and her husband Graham had just opened up. She was all bounce – something that you need in Richmond. She offered me a shower. There was tea in my room. I would live.

Everywhere I went I photographed sheep.

You need all your strength to tramp round Richmond. It is like a monumental rock cake with added fortifications. When all England has been eroded, Richmond will be there: proof against the nibbling tide. Everything about Richmond is surprising: everything you read, and everything you find out for yourself. It once belonged to France: Riche-mont. Richmond-on-Thames was named after it. The Lass of Richmond Hill was the daughter of a rich London solicitor who owned land there in Yorkshire who married the subject of his impassioned ode, and the song was first sung at Vauxhall Gardens. Byron's wife came from there. Cobbett appears to have missed it. A pity, because on market day it must be some spectacle still. In the eighteenth and nineteenth centuries it was the centre for farmers and manufacturers from all over North Yorkshire. You can imagine the noise and bustle in that high market square, wagons and horses clattering over the cobbles. Then the railway brought more trade. Today, you see it as a testing ground for four-by-fours. Even a Land Rover Discovery would find it tough. I tackled it on foot, my boots itching for battle, my bike at rest in a shed.

From my high crag at Pottergate, I descended to the town – only to go up again, for Richmond is shaped a little like a bowler hat or a Yorkshire pudding. You have to climb down from the rim before rising to the crown. It means, of course, that you see most of its splendours twice. Down there, squalled over by jackdaws and rooks, is Grey Friars tower, a grim excrescence with a high pointed arch at the bottom and blank Early English windows, turrets and finials at the top. It is Gothic gone mad: a grisly shell, and all that remains of the early monastery. It partly prepares you for the splendour of the Square. This is approached by intriguing alleys such as Finkle Lane. Cramped and climbing, you are suddenly released onto a shore of cobbles and – on a fine day – such a bowl of light that not even the castle, the obelisk and Trinity Church (all grouped together) can blot it out. The massive Georgian King's Head Hotel makes next door Woolworth look small – as it should. Altogether, however, you have the impression that Richmond has out-lived its Georgian heyday. I ate at a pub in Frenchgate, where the room was furnished with style – but the food was not.

The greatest feature of Richmond, after all, is the saucy Swale. I wandered down an unlit back street to the Falls. Somehow the dancing torrents seemed to catch and hold all the twilight that remained. Accompanied by this magical plaything of nature, I strolled along the riverside lawns, but lately cleared of the flood. The town stood silently above me, in effigy, in silhouette. And the laughing Swale danced on.

Between Richmond and Ripon, I especially enjoyed the splendid little Georgian market town of Bedale. I entered it by the village of Aiskew – a name to conjure with in these parts. Outside what I can only describe as a shop that dealt mainly in wooden objects, I spotted a dog-cart. I was tempted to buy it to draw behind my bike. Bedale itself has a wide, straight street, like Marlborough's. It has small, old-fashioned shops with names like Plews and Pocklington, and no sign of a supermarket. The butcher sold me a pork pie (homemade), told me his name was Fred when I asked him, smiled and said he envied me. (I had not been envied by a butcher before.) Mrs Ewart at the T.I.C. at the top of the town told me I should see the arboretum at Snape. I could stay at Kirlington if I didn't want to go all the way to Ripon that night. Fixed. I laid Elan to rest by a lamp post and made as if to enter the church. Before even arriving at the door, however, I spotted three adjacent stones to the memory of Askew, Ayscough and Askey. A name, as I said, to conjure with.

It was quite refreshing to read in the guide that 'there is nothing "Norman" to show at Bedale'. There has been a church there since Saxon times, but the one we see today is mainly thirteenth or fourteenth century. A great deal of church-building went on in this area following the havoc caused by the Scots, flush from their victory over Edward II at Bannockburn. The fortified tower is enough to frighten anyone. Inside, however, for all its reassuring solidity, it is ample, light and warm. Pairs of effigies lie prostrate at either side of the west end of the nave: two unknown knights and Brian FitzAlan, Lord of Bedale, 1243-1306 A.D., and his first wife Muriel. FitzAlan was a scion of the Earls of Richmond. There were FitzAlans in Shropshire and Montgomery – just as much a power in the land, defending our borderland against the Welsh. Moreover, thought I, Lady Anne Clifford, Countess of Cumberland, was also Countess of Pembroke, Somerset and Montgomery. What hierarchic can of worms had I opened here?

Moving into the greater light of the east end, my eye was caught by what looked like a giant's wooden money box with three hefty locks. The friendly vicar, still casting up his accounts after the early morning service, told me it was indeed an old form of safe. There is nothing like a good English parish church to help us make sense of our history. But the churches, like the history, are inexhaustible. I bowed to the knights as I left – thinking of their brothers lying stony-faced in Edvin Load (Worcs) and Aldworth (Berks). I had no time to ask the vicar about the assembled Askew, Ayscough and Askey in the churchyard; but I noticed in passing that the last died aged only eighteen.

Mrs Ewart of the T.I.C. was quite right about Thorp Perrow arboretum at Snape, of course. Jenny's Walk...Annabel's Walk...Henry's Island... The same affection is displayed here as in our churches. And dedication. And intimacy – even on a grand stage. Well, churches are, after all, largely avenues of stone. No asking here, however. There was no one else about. I had the whole earth and sky to myself. I say sky, because the emergent almond and cherry blossom constantly drew one's eye upwards to it on that beautiful day. It was cerulean – a colour favoured by designers like Adam for their ceilings in the great country houses of the eighteenth century. Lightness is all.

Nothing – neither in nature nor art – prepares you for Well. I knew it was there, on Mrs Ewart's recommended route. Approaching Well – a low-lying village as the name suggests – I had spotted the honey-stoned tower of the church, brilliantly picked out by the sun. I stopped and trained my binoculars on it. It was pure perpendicular. Only the farm buildings, I noticed as I went further along, exceeded the church in length; but they could not match it for height. It was the classic village set up: the church by the farm and their attendant farmhouse, cottages, post office and – in the old days – smithy and school. Now, of course, Well Hall Farm has almost outgrown the church – and most of the homes in the village are unrelated to either.

The road curled steeply to a line of cottages on the village's southern edge, presently a commanding view. There I met a man polishing his seat. It was a defining moment of my trip. Mike Holmes had bought Ivy Cottage, the last of the line. It was tiny, he said, but it was his. He had also bought the paddock opposite to preserve the view. He and his wife sat for hours on that seat. No wonder he was polishing it. Mike, a Leeds man, is a keen post-card collector and student of the village. He has postcards or photographs of the village at almost every stage of its modern development – and some illustrative material from earlier times. Overlooking his 'garth' above the church-centred village and Well Hall Farm, we discussed everything to do with Well: its old association with the Neville family, the advantages, the disadvantages... He showed me a splendid picture of the farm house cellar which was like a cathedral crypt. I trained my binoculars again and again over this beautiful honey-combed survival of old England. We agreed it had escaped ribbon development, except along one straight road to the north. Infilling, though apparently random, was relatively confined and pictur-esque – rather like the nursery of a very large family, cluttered, but still matching the manners of the main part of the house.

Kirklington, to which I now headed to spend the night, is another splendid patronal village. Like Dufton in Cumbria, it has a green, spacious and preserved with an air of untouchability. The freedom this gives is so precious it must be protected. Once lost, it can never be recovered. My room at Kirklea overlooked the church, whose tower even in the afternoon seemed washed in moonlight. It is a limestone song of praise. Beech trees rival it for height. Rooks fight for nesting places in their long, filigree boughs – and one bendy pine. In the morning, I scanned the wall memorials inside the church for news of its exalted past. There were Daltons and Wandesfordes and Priors linked to the Earldom of Kirklington and Hipswell who were large landowners in Kilkenny. An intriguing network of marriage gave them power over the church and the village, especially, it seems, in the eighteenth century.

On my way to Ripon – still skewering quick notes with my biro to a piece of card which I later lost – I remember writing: 'Some lord has had to rebuild his wall. It stretches for about two miles and is almost entirely built of cobbles placed here by hand by many men...'. It had been torn down in places by a few – and put back up. Lordie had had the last say. I remember reflecting that the men are dead, the lord that built it, too; but the wall lives on. And rooks build high in beeches on the estate, where rooks never built before.

I arrived in Ripon early, tethered Elan to a seat in the Square and stocked up at Morrison's with apples and Mars bars. 'Spend it while yer 'ere an' you've gorrit!', I overhead someone say. The commonalty of Ripon are saved by their cathedral. And by the man at the Gift Box nearby who sells everything from meerschaums to teapots and told me the best route to Fountains, via Studely Roger and Studely Royal.
'You'll enjoy that!' I did.

Durham has a chapel of Nine Altars; so does Fountains. Richmond has a curfew; Ripon has a hornblower. *'Except ye Lord keep ye cittie, ye Wakeman waketh but in vain.'* Ripon also has an obelisk, a monument to William Aislabie of Studely Royal, a perfect example of eighteenth century landowning man. Son of a politician and landowner with interests in the South Sea Company, he was in his time mayor of and M.P. for the town. Continuing the landscaping hobby of his father, he 'gardened' the ruins of Fountains Abbey for his own and our delight.

I do not know a dorter from a frater or a garde-robe from a conversorium, but Fountains captivated me. You drop down to it through fields farmed in the modern way with a noisy tractor and hedge flail fretting their way about the estate. There are some sheep – but not the 15,000 that there were in the heyday of the Abbey. Sturdy, high-energy ladies advance down the paths in windcheaters, slacks and sensible boots, making light of their age and the ravages of time. And then you see the whole wreck of this great ship of stone, sunk in a trough the size of the Pacific Mindanao Trench. You photograph it from the high shore for fear that, by the time you get down there, it may have gone. But it is no mirage, as the testing time that follows proves.

A powerful lot of leg-work is needed to see Fountains, lazy though your eye might be. The entrance fee (£4.50) is nothing to the cost in energy to reach the site. Viewing points along the trail help; but, in the end, you have to get down there. I took a short cut. What are bottoms for, but for sliding downhill?

It is the finest abbey ruin in the world, but built by earthy men. Twelve, originally. A Middle Age cricket team. The Prior and a handful of break-away monks from York. Did they and their followers put only piety into the building of this? Strength, I think; and a fierce determination. You forget you have a weak ligament when you see the possibilities here. It has the same implosive effect on the mind as the Rubaiyat of Omar Khayyam and the Gospel of St John. It is, of course, a poem of love. The joy of seeing it is somehow the same joy that the men must have felt who built it. A shared joy. A communion, regardless of time. A handshake with the poor masons and their labourers who placed it there, stone upon stone and arch upon repeated arch. Implosive and accumulative. They must have never tired of adding to the splendour. It takes your breath away. It took theirs, too. I put Fountains first because it stands first in my memory. It is past, present and future because, when many other monuments are gone, I am convinced it will still stand there.

I stayed at Bay Tree Farm, Aldfield, whence I flew with Elan back to Ripon Cathedral for evensong. It was unaccompanied, Tompkins and Tallis – an unalloyed delight. In the morning, strengthened, I set out for Pateley Bridge.

The road to Pateley Bridge and on to Grassington was like a long, slow crawl round the backside of the Dales. It had its uncomfortable moments.

It had its rewards. You do not quite know what to expect of this part of the anatomy of Yorkshire.

It looks like a straight road, the B6265, on the map, but I had to call on all my reserves of strength built up by leaving Elan in a shed and meditating in cathedrals in the past five days. I travelled so slowly with the wind blowing crossways over the moor that I was able to make notes – scribbling them in illegible squiggles with a biro on a piece of card which slipped easily into my pocket, and as easily out.

'Seeya', said the girl at the riding school where I asked about the ballet dancing balloons on the hill to my left. She knew as little about radar or satellite tracking stations as I.

'Memwith Hill – U.S. air base', she said. 'We don't know too much about 'em'. She smiled and got on grooming her horse. She was the prettiest girl I had seen in all Yorkshire.

'NIDDERDALE', says a sign. I photograph Elan in front of it for accomplishment.

'COLLIE DOG & BITCH FOR SALE, PUPS & PET LAMBS' at Nidderdale Lodge Farm.

'Oldest sweet shoppe in England 1827', announced itself next to a tea shop, opposite the library where I could park and lock Elan while I went for a cup of tea. This, at last, was Pateley Bridge. I might stay here. I might have to.

'Seeya now', said an elderly iron-grey gentleman, an ex-miner perhaps, who sat outside the chip shop, snuggling and wrestling with a firecracker terrier he told me he had just got from the RSPCA. I was struck by the radiant face of this man who, in addition to struggling to hold on to his dog, had obvious signs of Parkinson's.

Jenny Trigg and daughter Tib were pictured on a card in the paper shop. Pen-y-ghent. Celtic? I had a college friend called Trigg.

'Not far to Grassington', the lady in the shop told me.

'You're not walking? Lovely views.'

I walked the next four miles up a 16% hill. Everything had been a preparation for this, I told myself. All the oranges consumed in Lent. Just as you thought that was the last incline, there was another one ahead. Just as you thought that was the last hilltop house, there was another one too. You measure the incline by the angle of the roof. Cars, the same. A lorry is a good test. You can see the top of it dip after cresting the hill, then rise again… then roll on up to meet the clouds.

I was constantly entertained by sheep and lambs, plovers and curlews, calling back to them as they called to one another – or to me. You end up talking to sheep. The ridge of houses up here are clamped down with concrete. One, once splendid, long farmhouse had diamond paned windows but half an arched door bricked up, half an outside wall missing and an old mill stone somehow cut in two with only one half left. (Not like the mill stones, set on edge in concrete and proudly presented by the roadside, as you see in other parts.) Who lives in these lonely outposts of the Dales? KELD HOUSE 1642. That lifted my spirits. That must have been there in Cromwell's time.

'Grassington 7'. At Green How there was a quarry and, by the roadside, a heather garden in a mound of stones. 'NO WAGON TO ENTER THIS SITE BEFORE 5 A.M. There were signs of land mines, spoil heaps and underground passages with the odd brick arch like a red eyelid raised in the ground. It reminded me of the Stiperstones. A ewe with two lambs was looking intently up at a bedroom window of the house on the opposite side of the road. On the window ledge a tortoiseshell cat sat eyeing me and retreating slowly towards the open half of the window at the far end. The ewe, transfixed, stamped her foot. Ah, the lengths that a ewe will go to protect her offspring!

Caught in the crossfire of those trans-Pennine winds, I pushed my bike, gripping the back of the saddle as you do when helping a child to learn to ride. I was reduced to impotence. A ewe just about holds on to her wool up there; it hung like scarves from her neck. When would I be repaid my 16%? My legs had shrunk.

TOFT GATE. NOTICE OF OLD MILL AUTOS PENNINE RALLY

Traffic still went tilting up. It was a WW1 battle. A new house. How did the builder hold onto the tiles? Four plovers dipped, dipped and swung. D.v. they would survive and multiply. Their nesting-ground must be fairly undisturbed up there. The road started to go down. 16%. D.v. I would get my dividend. STUMP CROSS CAVES. Boys hurtling themselves about on trail bikes. RRRRRRH! The road went up again. I talked to a gimlet-eyed, cross fell ewe. Spotted a French letter by the roadside, shrunken in a trickle of rain. Someone must have been doing it in the cold. Two shock-coated farm dogs appeared like sweep's brushes tied end to end. HILL 1 IN 4, down to WELCOME GRASSINGTON!

Now I only had to skip to Skipton in the rain – a mere nine miles. A rainbow smiled on Kettlewell. I met, this Sunday morning, strings of cyclists cheerily pouring into the Dales, grinning to me as we passed. They had smiles which no amount of wind and rain could wipe off. They were colourful as the lads who ride out on the gallops at home. Downhill to Skipton, with its air of being an industrial smudge in a pastoral scene. Down to the castle and church ('Welcome!'); the paper shops, Morrison's and the downtown area where there might have been mills in the past and the canal... A few old men took home beans and fags in plastic bags. Skipton had gone flat on me. Ah, here came the station at last! My ticket to Huddersfield via Leeds was a mere £3.50. We took our place on the platform, Elan and I.

'How are you there?' said a young railwayman.

Everyone was so friendly. Whether it was my age, my look of being a happy clown with my colourful accoutrements, harking back to the days of vagabonds, I knew not. It might have been Elan. He has the spectral beauty of moonlight, as seen in the limestone tower of Kirklington Church, or the death-in-life face of the iron-grey gentleman at Pateley Bridge.

How was I here? I took it for a blessing. A miracle. A lucky sign.

Can you think of a more enticing destination than Appleby-in-Westmorland? It is more delectable than Dar-es-Salaam to me. For weeks before going I rehearsed the route – and I would be going in June, the time of wild roses and the even wilder gypsy Horse Fair happenings. Part of the excitement of going to Appleby is its 'otherness'. Like Rutland, Westmorland has defied the planners and retained its spiritual – if not its physical – identity. It is different. The heart of modern Cumbria beats more palpably to the left: the Lake District. The Eden Valley, however, is no less appealing. It nudges the Pennine Way and the hair-raising waterfalls like Cauldron Snout and High Force that mark the Durham boundary. And Appleby is no theme park. The gypsies have traditionally assembled there; and the local council has sensibly arrived at an accommodation, meeting them half way. There is plenty of common land, plenty of water in the river for the horses (and their riders) to splash about in, plenty of beer on tap, for at least a taste of an alternative way of life. And, like most natural phenomena – the northern lights for instance – it is not something you see every day. We are, after all, all travellers, just visiting. We may love our settled homes, our cultivated ways; but we are all curious about what other people do and how they live – the staple fair of television. What lies, more literally, just round the corner concerns us all. We are all gypsies at heart.

Suddenly, however – and only a week before setting off – I was seized by doubt. My heart, so eagerly set on this mission, failed me. Why, I asked myself, was I, who so earnestly believed in the settled life of the village – the community of the church, the farm and the school, physically and spiritually close-knit – seduced by what was probably only a mirage in my mind? After all, though the setting is the Eden Valley, I had not forgotten how wild the fells and the surrounding gills, moors and commons of old Cumbria can be. My OS map showed a Roman road and 'Fortlet' alongside the Carlisle to Settle railway. And where the Romans were yesterday, the MOD is today; for there is a huge emptiness to the north marked DANGER AREA in red. My eye lighted on a place beyond that called Knock Old Man. Where Cumbria runs into Durham and Northumberland can seem as inhospitable as the outback of Australia. I should, I decide, camp at a modest B & B in Bolton, to the west, and tip-toe to the Fair by Eden Grove and Eden Fields along what I took to be a green, safe, riverside path.

Walking promotes thought; cycling propels ideas. Uphill, downhill, you argue the toss with yourself. This northern region, you tell yourself, is only one of many areas of England that are totally distinct and, as it were, unabsorbed by the main body politic. They nurture people who are unimpressed by Westminster and 'what the papers say'. They have minds of their own. They may be heavily prejudiced, but they profess themselves resolutely independent and free of the tainted south. Is it, I wonder, to this breath of fresh air, this cold douche of reality at Appleby, that the gypsies hurry from the fantasies of Epsom only a week before. England, I suppose, has always had to come to terms with the accommodation of all sorts and conditions of men, from the time of Alfred and the Danes. More than her Empire, this has been the great success story of her history. It is therefore in Appleby that I may find Eden, quite literally.

You cannot avoid the castle as you come to Appleby by Colby Lane. It speaks of permanence as proudly at the south end of Boroughgate, the main street, as the church proclaims it demurely at the lower, north end. Somehow over the centuries they have severally come to terms with invaders of all kinds: the border raiders and the infidels. You think of York when you see the old street names: Bongate and Barrowgate, Shaws Wiend and Doomsgate. And you think, when you see the size of those ruddy sand-stone walls, of Jerusalem and the psalm which says *'Peace be within thy walls...* (Peace is only ever prayed for by people who have known strife.) and *'For thither the tribes go up..'*, you think of the constant flow of gypsies seek-ing accommodation on Fair Hill – and overflowing onto every available grass verge at that end of town. The Devil's Stewpot, Langland or Bunyan might have called it. The beer flows, the conversation and the money flow; the tradesmen and the dealers have a spree; the small farmers come down from the hills, shy collies to heel, to thumb their chins and smile at all that town tomfoolery.

In a downpour of rain such as only a June day in England can produce, I came in at the top of the town near Doomgate and walked purposefully on. I had come expecting to see gypsy boys and their horses bathing in the river. There were a few with the usual hang-dog look of tethered horses, standing under trees along the riverside path, waiting it seemed for their owners who had tethered themselves to a nearby pub. I went into the church.

Appleby church is everything that is English: it is old; new; intimate, grand; squat and spacious; preserved, restored; ceremonial, informal; com-pact but uncluttered; classy but welcoming; a beautiful treasure-house and open – for which we should all get down on our knees and be thankful, these days. It sits down town by the river, a little aloof from the secular goings-on of late twentieth century Appleby; but maybe it has always been so. Small border towns like this – one thinks of Bishops Castle – have always had more pub-goers than church-goers, situated as they are at the intersection of drovers' and other wayfarers' routes. (Shrewsbury is reckoned to have once had nearly as many churches as pubs within its walls – but few of the former are well-attended today.) Still, here in Appleby, there is a mission open at the back of the town, with a colourful banner which clearly says 'Jesus Lives.'

'They tried to get the devil out of me', said one young lady to her friends outside. Jesus would wait, but the junketing would not. 'No change given for the launderette', said a notice in the post office. 'Fifty pound notes not accepted', said another in the chip shop. So where was all the money coming from? And where was it going to? (The chip shop was answerable for most of the litter which extended beyond the town on the Penrith river.) I was glad to take a late evening walk by the river, from Bolton to Colby and round by Appleby again.

The river tells you all you need to know about Appleby; it holds it in its arms, and is the source of all goodness; its naissance and raison d'etre. In its long history it has succoured the farms, the churches and the schools on which all communities depend. It has also been its main defence. (It is reminiscent of York, Canterbury, Ludlow, Shrewsbury – indeed, most ancient and interesting settlements.) Men, I am tempted to say, make castles and stake out the farms; but women are more associated with rivers, churches and schools – hence their feminine nature and gender. We think of them as maternal and sources of nourishment and peace.

So, I returned again and again to the river and the church, finding every stick and stone of the latter especially interesting. For instance, when you enter the ancient porch with its dog-toothed arch, to see the memorial stone of Wilberforce Milner who died in 1838, aged one week. Forgetting the Normans for a moment, you scratch around inside your head for the dates of William Wilberforce who was born here; and you realize that the boy was probably named after him, just as after the war a popular name was that of Winston – another great deliverer.

I was escaping again from the incessant rain which left the whole of Appleby awash with water and mud. Even the colourful crowds began to look bedraggled and cheerless. Not quite hopeless – and still defiant – the gypsies sported Indiana Jones hats, high boots and long leather coats. They kept up the swagger – the secret of their success. The women wore fantastic head-pieces reminiscent of Persia as well as India, gold earrings the size of hoops and every kind of ring, bangle or stud on the rest of their persons. They stood out among the men, often being taller, more proud in their bearing, but less willing to display the gold in their teeth.

Litter flowed in the gutters, needing an Eden Task Force operating from over the bridge to clear it up every night. Beer flowed in the pubs. One had a dress code: no jeans… no young persons in large groups… Nearer the bridge, however, were the dark, squat, back-slapping, good-time people, all in leather jerkins and wide-awake hats with fancy ribbons, swigging beer, flashing their rings and slapping their hands. Gypsies touch each other more than gorgios. At this end of town – low town, you might call it – the police were out in force. They stood around with their arms folded, creating a presence in brilliant yellow jackets and formal helmets. Patrol cars constantly crossed the bridge. Tourists leaned over the sandstone parapet. Somebody said a gypsy dude had unloaded wife and kids from his Mercedes and driven it into the river. Showing off! Silver, it was! Did he remember to shut the doors? Most of the coach-loads of trippers from Gateshead and Lancashire took refuge in the Copper Kettle for slow filtered coffee or fished around the Arcade and the Public Hall for a second-hand book or a hand-painted tea pot (Art Deco: but would it pour?) to take home.

But, after all, if you have any sense, you end up in the church. There, the architecture sorts the centuries out; history is laid before you in a nice, manageable text. There, you learn that the organ dates from the time of William Byrd, John Bull and Orlando Gibbons, and was a gift in the seventeenth century from Carlisle Cathedral. 'It needs cleaning – but we'll repair the roofs of the two side aisles first which will cost about fifty thousand pounds and make such a lot of dust'. I said how much I would love to hear the organ played, imagining it to sound as sweet and silvery as it looks. 'I'm afraid you'll have to buy the CD.' (No thanks.) 'There's a memorial to Lady Anne Clifford, you know… There were ten gypsy christenings this week… Only one in the Sunday service, though… All the grown-ups wanted to dabble their fingers in the font… They couldn't understand why the vicar didn't give them a candle as well as the child… "Come round to the house after the service", he said… But they didn't, of course… George Washington's brothers went to school in Appleby, you know… Half brothers they were, I think… I taught history at the grammar school myself for ten years…'

All this nectar I had from a little lady humming bird of a guide. Later, I remarked to a Cranford-type sister that the church is evidently very active in its support of the leprosy mission and the Uganda appeal. 'Yes', she said with a faint, sweet, wintery smile, 'but we're all getting older.'

Now I tackled Anne Clifford, Countess of Pembroke, who spent her life putting to rights the wrongs of her inheritance and restoring and beautifying this church and a large cross-section of England in the process. It was her custom to reside at fixed times at each one of her six castles while dispensing her charity and hospitality, but *'never tasting wine or physic'*. John Donne said she knew well how to discourse of all things, from predestination to slea-silk. She died at Brougham Castle in 1676, but was buried in the vault which she had built for herself in Appleby church. Lady Anne, who was Countess of Somerset and of Montgomery as well as Pembroke, first married the Earl of Dorset, by whom she had three sons and two daughters. The husband and sons all died young. *'Smallpox'*, she wrote, *'so martyred my face that it confirmed more and more my mind not to marry again, though ye providence of God caused me after to alter that resolution.* By her second husband, she had no children. *'The marble pillars of Knowle in Kent and Wilton in Wilts were to me oftentimes but the gay arbour of anguish.'* There were wrangles over her run-down estates; but on the death of Henry Clifford, fifth and last Earl of Cumberland, they reverted to her under the provision of her father's will. 'Her passion', says the Dictionary of National Biography, 'for bricks and mortar was immense.' Her castles at Skipton, Appleby, Brougham, Brough, Pendragon and Bandon Tower were all restored. She provided the almshouses for the people of Appleby which stand outside her favourite church.

Back at the bridge, where had been lines of piebald horses, there was only Laura, a two-year-old beauty that surpassed anything I had seen all week. Her boy sat sideways on her back, airily showing her off. She was the centre of everyone's attention. Small children eagerly reached up to her proud head and slid their hands down the lower part of her neck. She was not just stately, she was statuesque.

'How much?' I asked of the boy.

'Seven an' a 'alf', he replied without moving a muscle or turning a hair. 'I've got six more like 'er at 'ome.'

So he was probably no more a Romany than I… Did he mean seven and a half thousand, do you suppose?

'She's lovely', I sighed, knowing that he knew I was not likely to buy. And that was Appleby. Quality rubs shoulders with trash.

June 10, Sunday, and I was off to Soulby, Great Asby and the villages beyond. A fitful sun lit up the fells, those houseless hills that support stone walls and sheep, marked on the map as a DANGER ZONE. Near a farm entrance, I found a man scything grass. He was nearly hidden in the cow parsley – a little speck of agricultural history. I could tell he was a happy little man by the way he went about his work. I wondered whether to stop or not. Would he want to be interrupted? Would he have anything to say? I decided that to pass by would be like overlooking a silver sixpence spotted by the roadside. He belonged to my youth, when I too wielded a scythe. I parked the car a safe distance away, and strolled towards him. He smiled and turned to me. 'Nice morning.' His face shone, the sun shone – even the blade of the scythe, well-wetted, shone. Resting it on its handle, he smoothed his brow with his band. I told him about my common interest. 'Not many of us left, now', he said. He looked appreciatively at his scythe. 'You have to keep it well wetted.' The whetstone almost sprang from his trouser pocket to his hand, rhythmically swiping the blade several times with a sound that reminded me of pheasant chicks cheeping in the grass. Almost of their own accord the stone returned to his pocket and the scythe to its task.

'Rhythm is the thing', I said knowledgably. 'And minding you don't clout a stone', he grinned. We were getting on famously.

'Can I take a photo of you?' I asked, running back to the car.

'Of course', he said. 'A little bit of history!' He read my mind.

My tenses all jumbled up by this sudden encounter with primitive agriculture, I travelled on to Great Asby where I found the Rutter Falls. Excuse for further photography. Sudden jolt in geography. I thought black swans belonged to Australia. After Kirby Stephen – the church there combines Anglicanism with Roman Catholicism – I headed for the free range common sense of the fells. The road to Middleton in Teesdale took me to the border of County Durham, beyond which I decided not to pass. I was in an area of outstanding natural beauty – High Force, with high force winds – where the only buildings apart from the stone walls are shelters for sheep and even the prevalent ash has a struggle to grow. But I was captivated by the wild call of the curlew and the alarm peep-peeping of the oyster catchers as well as peewits and black-headed gulls. They played havoc with my binocular vision, skidding in and out of view like bats in the twilight. Then, just as you think you have focused on one and tracked it to earth, it is lost in the rushes. The curlew especially performs this vanishing trick with gurgles of delight.

I spotted a gully or a ghyll with a ewe and two black-spotted lambs photogenically placed. I crept along the wire-topped wall to catch them with the camera unawares. A wily ewe twenty yards away called a warning to her lamb. All my stealth was in vain. My picture will be of a ruck of scabby limestone round the rim of an old pit containing the remains of a car, registration G893...

I have been in a landscape little changed since Cobbett's, Washington's, Wilberforce's – even Roman times. A landscape incapable of change. A landscape given over to foxes, birds of prey and sheep. A landscape so bitten down that there is no meat left on the bone. A soldier's playground and the last workplace of the hardiest farmers in the land. Nature revives it each spring with the cries of peewits, curlews, oyster catchers and lambs – all eerily alike. The summer sun casts romantic cloud shadows over it. Autumn might be a fine time to see it; but you might sooner die than live there in winter. On these fells the wind never dies.

Back on the roads round Dufton and Knock, gypsies – mostly old and apparently single, with only one spare horse – trundle home. But where is home? At Dufton post office I had tea on the green. Opposite was a range of Georgian-style houses with arched doorways which speak of the days when even the doctor had a carriage and the parson lived in competition with the squire. But where was the church? It is some miles away at Knock, where, I was told, the monks travelling round with St Cuthbert's body came to rest and built a church. At Dufton there is a ghyll, where I saw we were on a St Bees sandstone deposit *'similar to that of the Nile...on rocks showing that a broad river flowed through a desert plain millions of years ago.'*

I gathered up my bike and my belongings and returned for the last time to the town where, on the outskirts, many unsettled ponies were herded in a field, disorientated like me. Many more were left tethered at the roadside, patiently hanging their heads. They looked as if they had been forgotten. A few jaunty gyppos with their vardos, dogs and acquired horses, still stuttered down the hill. An army of council workers, like foot soldiers with brooms, swept up the mess in the town. One bungalow dweller was doing his bit himself. There is nothing like Appleby to persuade you of the transitoriness of life. It is like a short fugue – one of the strictest forms in music – played annually for the delight, mainly, of the performers themselves. There are a set number of themes – the renewal of old friendships, the making of new; the sale and exchange of horses and other possessions; the celebration of summer and the unconstrained chance to show off in the open air. It is formal and traditional; but, within set rules, there is scope for endless experiment and surprise. It is like the waves produced by the constant fording of the river by spirited horses and their unfettered riders by the little town bridge. It is only a bit of buck and fizz. The rhythm of life goes on.

In seeing Appleby, I have seen more than the Fair. I have seen England: the Merrie England of the twinkling scythe and the long, far call of the curlew in a danger zone still, ironically, undisturbed – an England that the Countess of Pembroke strove to protect. An England where past is present, and the future will take care of itself.

A long, long trail awinding . . .

VIRGIN DERBYSHIRE

MERCIA, Wessex, Northumbria – and the rest... How formative were those early building blocks – and how fundamental! At Little Ness, we knew about Angles, Saxons and Jutes; Boadicea rode into our chilly classroom, wreaking havoc with her sword-blades sprouting from her chariot wheels. So we knew about the Iceni; but we knew nothing of the Belgae, Brigantes, Regenenses and the other early tribes. We knew about Alfred and his efforts to form a United Kingdom supposedly called England; his heroic stand against the Viking invaders; but we little realised how costly and extensive the Danelaw was. It even included Derbyshire. Small wonder, then, that it seemed at this late stage in life a strange and dangerous place to be.

Man had walked on the moon, cloned sheep and cracked the internet before I discovered Derbyshire. Brought up in nearby Shropshire with bikes, ponies and traps as our favoured modes of transport, I little knew what wonders lay between the 'Black Country'of the Potteries which stretched north of Birmingham to Stockport and Manchester in the west and Sheffield, Huddersfield and Leeds in the east. Everywhere north of Derby was deemed to be black. Lichfield was the centre of our diocese, but we never went there. We knew about Wedgwood and Coalport. The Liverpool to Manchester Ship Canal featured in our geography books. Sheffield was where the knives came from. Shrewsbury had some kinship with Derby through the railway and Rolls Royce. Buxton was a Spa and the Peak District was a then new National Park – both much needed from the sound of things. I didn't think I would ever take leave of my senses and visit Derbyshire. Thank God for the ignorance and folly of youth, I say; it renders age rich and wisdom is, like the best good wine, kept till now.

So it was that on Monday, the twenty-second of April 2002, I found myself on one of Richard Branson's Virgin trains running from Reading to Derby via Birmingham. 'City of a thousand transit vans', I noted in my diary. 'Leave New Street 16.00; Burton Bass, 16.30; a field of Herefords, ditto Aylesbury ducks, ditto dandelions...' There must have been some country-side between the grim buildings left over from Victorian times – one of which posed the question in large black letters on a shining white back-ground: WHAT IS TECHNOLOGY WITHOUT IMAGINATION? and did not stay for an answer. I was told by a fellow traveller that that might be the last time I would see that splendid name Bass, as elegantly inscribed as that of Kelloggs – both models of cursive handwriting – as the firm had been taken over or swallowed up, or whatever happens to old landmarks in this age of flux. 'The Rockies may tumble, Gibraltar may crumble', I hummed to myself, uncertain of either the tune or the words.

I was tipped out, with my bike – sole occupant of the guard's van – at Derby and put in a centripetal spin on the ring road, trying to find the A52 to Ashbourne, so clearly marked on my hand-held map. 'It's down there somewhere', a harassed pedestrian told me. Steel girders prevented any unauthorised road crossing so you had to find a set of traffic lights – 'Return to Go' – and hope that you did not find yourself back in Jail. (All railway towns – Reading, Shrewsbury, Derby especially – have or had great stone jails.)

Miraculously, all those concentrically travelling cars disappeared and I found myself, traffic-free, on my way to Ashbourne, airily disregarding Kirk Langley and Brailsford, determined to see what my guide book said Johnson, Boswell, Moore, Rousseau, Canning, George Eliot and Izaak Walton all revelled in: *'all knew the lovely roads to Ashbourne, for all of them lived or stayed here, and wrote here or put this country in their books'*. Night was closing in when I dropped in at the Plough.

The bar-tender at the Plough – a lady with a small child and a party of admirers in the snug – did not pay me much attention. I was given a key and a berth for my bike and left to find my way around this interesting, rambling public house of many doors. Trying to retrace my steps to my room, I twice had to ask the young couple playing pool for help. Play was willingly suspended, along with disbelief, and I confidently set out to look round the town. 'You have two supermarkets', I observed on my return. 'Four', they said, and got on with the game. I had not walked further than the bridge over the bourne – the Dove, I supposed – but the reflections of shop and street lights as well as the moon in a clear sky set my heart dancing at the thought of a fine morrow and a clear run to Buxton with Tissington to relish on the way. Meanwhile, back in my obscure but comfortable room, I made myself familiar with Dr John Taylor, friend of Dr Johnson, who nested in Church Street and received his distinguished visitors there in summer but overwintered in the south. It would really be something to step, literally back into the eighteenth century in the morning and see, almost unaltered, the old almshouses, the Elizabethan grammar school, and the 17th century brick house to which Dr Johnson came for many a holiday with his old school-fellow, the rector of Market Bosworth and St Margaret's, Westminster. *'Boswell tells us that he was like a hearty English squire with the parson added.'* So says Arthur Mee and goes on: *'When the Duke of Devonshire arrived to dine with the doctor, the coachman was ordered to drive twice round the grounds to give a good impression of their size.'*

Nothing illustrates more clearly what I see as the schizoid nature of the English than Arthur Mee. Here is this marvellous guide to Derbyshire, first published in 1937 but updated, emphasising the beauties of Church Street and the church itself, 'the Cathedral of the Peak', its monuments, *'for which thousands come to Ashbourne'*, and many delights besides, and I was probably the only visitor to the town that night aware of – nay, transfixed by – the gospel he preached. I could hardly sleep; in the morning I would set out before breakfast to explore Church Street where, even now, the good doctors, Boswell and Walton – or their ghosts – might be seen in animated and admiring conversation that would hold the attention of the egalitarian Rousseau or the impressionable Duke.

And it was so. In Church Street you leave behind the transitory world of one-stop stores and take-aways and enter the real, on-going, enduring world of upholstery, ironmongery, the solid architecture of banks and solicitors, schools and, of course, the cure of souls. And at the end of it all, a farm: Dr Taylor's farm, perhaps. How very fundamental is that farm!

On a postcard home – picturing St Oswald's church – I wrote: 'Just another church? It rivals St Mary Redcliffe. Set among beeches, just feathering into leaf, drifts of daffodils and dandelions, *'a large and luminous place'*- said Boswell – it has everything. Too much for a postcard'.

Two shire horses groomed each other, biting the winter scurf off their legs, head to tail by the churchyard wall, so close we were to nature here. An elder – layman, missionary, churchwarden caretaker, local historian – told me all that anyone could tell in ten minutes. I marvelled at the windows and monuments inside – and at the perseverance of the priest who seemed to be conducting a service for himself. God smiled on the stained glass; and on the *'little white figure of a child of six summers set here in marble'* along with the alabaster and Purbeck effigies of the Cokaynes, *'one of whom was with King Henry VIII on the Field of the Cloth of Gold'*, disinterestedly.

Before I reached Buxton at three o'clock, I had scribbled another p.c. 'Another church, Elizabethan Hall, TEAS!' A little culvert ran along the street, as at Bourton-on-the-Water. I dropped my apple, so dunked it in the culvert and picked a piece of watercress to go with it. A spot of rain. An accident on the hill out of Bentley. A young motorcyclist must have clipped the side of a van overtaking downhill. He lay like an animal by the kerb, the machine askew on the road. A single policeman assisting and directing traffic. Buxton 16 London 142!

I was blown to Buxton by a south wind, airily eliminating the miles with Elan. It was like finding a good thermal in a glider; onward and upward we flew. The increasing distance from London was as reassuring as the close-ness of the Peak. Poor London! Elan has eighteen gears, but I use only three. It is a mystery to me how the others work. A galaxy of gears! The Plough, Cassiopeia and Orion are my familiars. What need have I of the Nereids and the squinty little Pleiades, or those other star clusters of steel (the pride of Raleigh – and Britain) between my legs?

Between plunges downhill and sudden ascents I dwelt in the plain, thankful to rest my non-steel legs and exercise my shrivelled wits. I began to study stone walling. How is it done? Like the fashioning of crop circles, you never catch anyone doing it. Is there some sort of grammar or prosody that a dry stone waller has to learn? At first I thought: ah, you lay all the larger, longer stones at the base. But there were outcrops of larger ones sometimes in the middle – or at the top. Yes, there was nearly always a kind of cornerstone, a 'big boy' at the base somewhere along the line, but at no regular interval. The more you look, the more haphazard it seems. Sheer rule of thumb genius! You become mesmerized. You see the ghosts of thou-sands of proud men who laid millions of stones all over Derbyshire with their bare hands for very little pay – so much per thousand stones, or so much per thousand yards? – all individually, believing, no doubt, that they would stand the test of time. They have! But, just as you never see the cre-ator god who builds them, you never see the insensate devil who destroys them. Human erosion, I call it – more destructive than any natural force. In many places, the walls were breached – toppled by some all-steel satanic force. They were like giant molars mouthing the air with no binding and nothing left on which to bite. They were placed there by a beautiful econo-my: the waste, no doubt from the quarries which everywhere in the north provided fine stone for fine houses. The landowners, seeing the benefits of enclosure, shrewdly noticed a use for the spoil. 'Hey, lads, string this lot together!' Trees were scarce, hedges non-existent. 'Tha'll keep warm; stone'll keep in the sheep and keep out the wind.' Q.E.D. The logical geometry of the countryside! Occasionally I saw a single king-stone stooping in the middle of a line that must have once been a school of stones: the old headmaster hanging on, his pupils and his purpose gone. Once, I saw a board by a new wall which gave the name and telephone number of the phenomenon who built it. O rare defender of the faith! I should have made a note of him.

Buxton by three o'clock! Buoyed by self-worth – but not worth much else – I entered a second-hand bookshop, spotted C F Tunnicliffe's Shorelands Summer Diary (first edition), promised to pay when I returned home if the bookseller would post it, bought a card at the Post Office and – still pleased with myself – sped on to the Opera House. Certain things you must give priority. It is a let-down externally. Internally it is a rose and gilt Edwardian excess. It has cost a fortune to restore – 'and still they haven't done the floor!' someone told me. I saw 'The Lavender Hill Mob', a farce adapted from the film of that name by one of the actors and brilliantly performed. I slept at Stoneridge beside the Park, very comfortably, breakfasted and – onwards and upwards – pedalled on to the Peak. Tomorrow is another day; but in Derbyshire it is even more so.

I was intent on escaping from humanity and his unnatural habitations, to some idealized free zone such as the old navigators imagined – not quite of this world. My voyage was relatively uncharted. I did not really keep a log. Bits of paper, scribbled on as the thought occurred, were stuffed in my pocket one minute and gone with the wind the next. I sang like a child: 'The Kangaroo from Kathmandu' (words and music by myself) and adaptations of Masefield ('*I must go up to the hills again...To the peewit's way and the curlew's way where the wind's like a whetted knife...*' The wind was still southerly – '*Blow bonny breeze my lover to me..*' I saw and heard curlew, skylarks and swallows that I rarely see at home; but the plaint of the plover was absent from this mainly unploughed earth. (I counted perhaps two cultivated fields on the whole trip – and one seemed devoted to rhubarb.) I paused by a roadside shrine to Michael, 23, killed in a motorbike accident;

and by another to the Virgin Mary. I finally fetched up at Hayfield, *'on the threshold of the mighty range of Kinder Scout'*, (Arthur Mee's words) where I felt, as a farmer's son, I had really come into my own.

Leaving Elan in his stable at The George, I set out next morning on foot. Hayfield was half asleep. Only the sun was wide awake on this glorious spring morning, the 24th April, the anniversary of the mass Protest by the Ramblers Association which secured the inalienable right of Tom, Dick and Harry to roam over Kinder Scout and led to the creation of the High Peak National Park. I was warming to my history – our history. We all walk by our own effort, putting one foot in front of the other by our own painful measured, modest strength, like pilgrims, however we may feel united with our brethren – especially at the end. There is no room for schizophrenia here; no room for doubt; no retreat; thoughts, feelings and actions are all bent to one aim – the summit. No mountaineer, myself, I can readily see why a successful climb is accompanied by such joy. Throughout my trip I had the feeling of breaking new ground. Kinder is only 2,088 ft – just eligible to be considered a mountain – but it is pioneer special. No matter how many people may have climbed it before you; no matter how many cheerful but tired souls you meet or pass, you are recreating for yourself a very special event. You are making a point. You are staking a claim. The mountain streams and delightful waterfalls continually refresh your eyes and persuade your mind that the world is new.

Kinder is the apotheosis of the peak. It is all downhill – and a following, northerly wind – from there. The actual descent seems longer and harder than the climb. The sun is going down over that broad, vacant sheet of water, the reservoir; a young ewe with her first lamb was holed up in a heathery coomb; a red grouse strikes a death-rattle note; one's solitariness is emphasised; you are the last of the tribe. You feel privileged, carrying all its collective responsibilities. 'Please keep to the designated path.'

Just on the edge of town, a man is building a wall. It is pink, beige and almost purple in the lowering sun. It is only a small garden wall, but beautiful. You enquire about the stone. Was it Delabole, from Cornwall, perhaps? 'Nah, joost from roond aboot', said the man. 'Him's what we call a joompa, oota the river tha!'

126

His wife was helping him to tidy up – proud of her man and his job.

'Churchill built a wall', I said, waving goodbye. 'In his garden at Chartwell.'

'Yo're the secon' one who's towld me that t'day!'

I was, after all, only one of the crowd.

I had high hopes of Chapel-en-le-Frith, my next port of call; but, oh, the perils of literacy! I had read that it was a 'sturdy rather than picturesque' old market town. It – or its people – had a reputation for independence. William Bagshawe, a nonconformist minister, was ejected from the living of Glossop in 1662 and spent the rest of his life working in the wildest parts of the Peak. He is honoured with a memorial in the church at the top of the town which is dedicated to St Thomas à Becket. It is known that the first church here was a chapel built by the men who worked in the Peak Forest – shadowy figures still speaking Norman French.

After getting tangled up in the Industrial Estate City of Ferrodo (famous for brakes for over a century) I found myself on the ring road with a super-market out of town. What price this? I found a helpful newsagent. He flung an arm. 'Yer oright, guv, theer's the street!' The street is steep – and a rev-elation. There are joinery and hardware shops and an English-speaking tourist information centre, just opening for the season, anxious to tell me about well-dressing. Excited, I aimed a camera at shop-fronts old in story. But there was hardly anyone about. Such people as I saw in the street were heading downhill to the superstore, worried-looking, afraid to be seen. The sun was out, but the ladies all had headscarves on. The angle of the street cut out the light. But there was just enough for me to read: Vecchia Italia Pizzeria; El-Amin Indian takeaway; Goe Casadinos Hairdresser; Piccolo Mondo; Deli Zanussi; Chinese August Moon (Fish and Chips). I turned on my heel and rode out of town singing 'Piccolo Mondo Deli Zanussi' and other such tripe. Chapel-en-le-Frith was supposed to be one of the gate-ways for walkers to the hills. Still, it had given me words for another Jabberwocky-type song – a genre perfected by the English. I was heading downhill (Winnats Pass!) to Castleton to cool off in the caves.

I might not have gone to Castleton but for the fact that, on one of the occasional uphill stretches of my journey, I fell in with Farmer Mortenshaw. A land-rover drew up and he got out to look at me and his sheep. There is no one like a farmer – think of Cobbett or A G Street – for making enquiries and penetrating your reserve. Northern farmers, especially. But this was the first one I had met. He complimented me on my age and spir-it. Might do it himself, one day. Yes, the sheep were oright, but they'd bin through bad times. Yes, there was a lot o' construction about. Oh, he knew the quarrying business from the inside; he'd studied excavation. 'Yo goin' to the Caves? Left by the Wanted Inn, twenty minutes , careful doon Winnats Pass.' He was a busy man. Proud man. Local councillor, no doubt. But he had time to talk. He smiled.

I could have killed myself on that Pass – it had more hair-raising bends and blind drops than the Horseshoe Pass in Wales. (Dropped handlebars and a loose helmet didn't help.) I was emboldened by two bikers at the top – Laurel and Hardy – who introduced themselves from under their helmets and face-shields. They were resting on their way back to Stockport after making the ascent. Their bikes were twins – Nortons or Titanics – and under their alien black leathers they seemed to have a tender skin. They were buddies – escapees from the tyranny of Greater Manchester. 'Go for it', they said. Hurtling down the precipice that is Winnats Pass, I did not have time to reflect on the healing power of those Derbyshire hills, but I have since done so. Since the eighteenth century, when England's schizophrenia began, men, and even women in hooped skirts, have come here for refreshment from the very sickness they had brought upon themselves. If England has ills, it also has the natural antibodies to cure them.

Laurel and Hardy were a marvellous comedy duo, but Richard and Michael were even better. I found them in the Caves. Nothing but a capital C will do. The whole defile, where the earth seems to have been turned upside by natural forces long before Man came along with his bucket and spade, is called Hope Valley. It is wonderfully spectacular on the surface. How much more so underneath! Mr Mortenshaw told me about the aptly named Speedwell Cavern, but not the earlier Blue John. There is a kind of toll-house on one side of the road where you get your ticket – and the inevitable cafeteria foregathering shop on the other. You discard all unwanted objects, silently, shiftily checking your pulse and wondering whether you should make your will. It is a two hundred odd feet drop, single file, down as many steps, you are warned. There is a strange camaraderie induced by fear perhaps; but that is quickly extinguished by the youthful high spirits of Richard, our nimble, ebullient guide. He is a university graduate, trained in geology and, evidently handy with a rope. (Light bulbs have to be replaced way above the stalactites sometimes, and the best Blue John specimens are often the most inaccessible.) You feel safe with Richard; and his enthusiasm for geology is matched by a young man from California who has the gift of stretching the information like chewing gum to unbelievable lengths; tuned and practiced, as well as practical, scientific minds generating intense interest.

It is impossible to convey the marvellous gothic beauty of these Caves; one is tempted to say, unearthly, comparable only to dreams and out-of-body experiences. Let the photographs speak for themselves. But I must try to capture the spirit at least of our two marvellous guides. (I, who am usually reluctant to part with money for information which I consider to be freely available through the senses.) These guys were young, athletic, knowledgeable and wonderfully entertaining professionals. Witness Michael 'legging' the boat at Speedwell through the cramped, dimly lit channel with a bare three feet of water below and trillions of tons of rock overhead, cracking (good) jokes as he went. I saw him later swigging a soft drink. He would be doing the trip again in an hour. Same freshness, same worthwhile commentary salted with good-boyo cheek. Lucky England, to have such down-to-earth treasures –old and young together – as these!

It was sad to have to leave the heathery heights of Kinder Scout, opened to public tramps like me by Benny Rothman just seventy years ago, and to descend to the cities of the plain. I knew that I would not have the company of the curlew, red grouse or lone ewe nursing her lamb in the coomb. Those 'cities' included Eyam, whose story is branded on every Englishman's brain; Matlock, which does not sound very exciting but is; Wirksworth – the homestead of Weorc; and Duffield where, thank goodness, a train took me and my bike to Derby and another one took us home. Not, however, before I had experienced many surprises which, at the time and on reflection, lead me to think Derbyshire and its people a model for the building of Jerusalem – if only we were serious about it – in our land.

You cannot fault Eyam. The shadows of the past are as much a part of the place as are the yews of the beautiful, sombre church. Coach loads of visitors thronged the museum and the little tight streets, but I headed for the church. I found a lady guide whose father was organist here for many years. She showed me Parson Mompesson's chair in the chancel, which was miraculously discovered in a Liverpool auction room, restored and returned. The chair is the man. Just as you could see the lady's father seated at the organ, you could see Mompesson working at his sermon in his chair.

Back at the car park and the museum, a party of rowdy schoolboys had discovered an echo in the loo. I headed for a little upstairs café which I had spotted before. I was the only one asking for lunch at two o'clock. The waitress was very understanding. The background music intrigued me: very easy on the ear, Sunday afternoon on the river stuff.

'What is it?' I asked.

'Enya.' I felt I was supposed to know Enya.

I ate my jacket potato, cheese and strong Derbyshire onions.

'Who?' I asked again.

'Enya.'

'Before my time.'

'Naw, she's recent.'

'Greek?' I hazarded.

'Naw.' She showed me the CD case.

'Yes', I said, 'Greek, dark, seductive.'

Poor girl, she got fed up with me.

I returned to the museum where the rowdies had tired of the echo and (perhaps because of it) caught up with the past.

' How much for one old child?' I asked, teasingly.

'One pound, please.' The ladies at the ticket booth were helpful volunteers. Eyam people are like that. If you don't remember anything else, you remember their patient, sympathetic smiles. But I don't like museums which are geared to teachers' and children's needs with their dressed-up papier-mâché figures and potted histories. I saw more in that chair of Mompesson's in the church.

I left Eyam with its sad echoes of the Plague minded to rest overnight at Bakewell; but Bakewell had no room; I travelled on to Matlock. I had plenty of time to dwell on the terrible irony that it was through a bale of cloth sent from London to Eyam's tailor that the disease had been visited upon the village in September 1665. Cloth was his livelihood. The first of the Plague victims was the journeyman who opened the box containing the cloth. Death stalked the village for many months; 259 people were buried in fields and gardens around. William Mompesson and his nonconformist colleague Thomas Stanley saw the scourge through to the bitter end. Mompesson, a widower now, left the village for a living in Nottinghamshire, but Stanley remained at Eyam till he died in 1670, spurned by the remainder of the flock for his nonconformity.

I cherish Matlock as one of the great surprises of my life. I somehow knew what to expect at Eyam; I knew what Bakewell was – old and agricultural; but nothing prepares you for the physical magnificence of Matlocks-in-the-Plural: Matlock Bath, Matlock Dale, Matlock Bridge, Matlock Town and Matlock Bank. I pitched up at Matlock Bank.

My diary notes (those that had not gone with the wind) tell me that I arrived late that evening at 80 Matlock Bank (or it could have been 800) and I christened it Matlock Summit. From my eyrie I could see about half of a ruined castle, Gothic as that of Otranto, pear blossom, cherry blossom, lilac and forsythia, high cumulus and a Reckitts blue sky. I could not stay, tired though I was, cooped up there. Snatching up my camera but forgetting my notes, I went out on the town. Earlier, someone had stopped halfway up the bank – steep and dangerous to cars, I should have thought – and asked me the way to the Council offices car park. 'Dunno', I said in my best Shropshire accent. Now, two hours later, I found both the car park and the offices. 'CONSELUDO BONO' it said – which I took to mean Good Counsel – over the main entrance to the Town Hall. The heavy oak door was open. I should have walked in. 'What's the monument of stone past the old factory chimney over there', I asked my landlord when I returned. 'Smedley's Hydro', he said, as if I should know. 'And the castle?' 'Smedley's folly', he said with a wince. I was to learn more about Smedley next day.

Even the guide book seemed to think I should know about Smedley as one should know about Arkwright at Comford down below. Yes, he was a hosiery manufacturer. But how did a hosiery manufacturer lug that Roman Empire of stone up this steep hill? He had fallen ill, it is said, and decided to build a spa, for the treatment of his own, his workers' and the ailments of the wider world. It is obvious, when you think about it. Stone was there in abundance; the workers needed work; the world needs health.

It is only when you cycle out to Matlock Bath, however, that you realise what a magnet this place must have been for the Victorians. The River Derwent glides through a sylvan ravine like a painted snake. The Victorians, with their ailments and their artistic sensibilities, were always in awe of natural masterpieces: Tintern, Bettys-y-Coed or Venice itself. They could lay down their paint brushes and admit defeat. Ruskin, that great advocate of harmony and healing between the gentleman artist and the downcast artisan, admired Matlock. I vulgarly called it in my diary 'the cleavage of the broad bosom of England'. I went on my way singing the Barcarolle from the Tales of Hoffman and Red (turned to Green) River Valley and Farewell my darling I must leave thee, and telling myself that there is nothing more beautiful than water flowing over stone, enhanced by natural light.

I had not gone far up the hill when I met a man feeding hens. Relaxed, old enough to be retired, he welcomed me to his patch of ground by the roadside with a few hen-huts and appliances scattered around. It was not his habitation, he explained; he just kept it on for a hobby. He reminded me of my father who was never so happy as when throwing corn for his hens. You pick up a few eggs, freshly laid; you don't think of the cost of the corn, wastefully lodged in the weeds. Make the hens work for it, he would say. 'See that zinc gate just up the road', said my friend. 'On the right. This road divides the millstone grit on the left from the limestone on the right. Go through that gate, cross the field, and you'll see a sight for sore eyes.' My eyes were not sore, but I followed his advice. There, laid out like a moon-scape, was Dene Quarry, stretching as far as I could see. There, under my nose, was a memorial larger than any I had seen before to one working man: *'Don Harris…who on the 6th May 1942 walked onto this hillside with wheel-barrow and hand shovel and started Dene Quarry, spent all his working life here and researched the ancient history of the area and gave his knowledge for the ben-efit of all.'* With that to inspire me, how could I fail to make Wirksworth by noon?

You wake up when you come to Cromford. It is suddenly there, round the corner, like a babe in a cradle of rock. If it were not for Arkwright's Mill and his Mansion – and of course the tourist attractions – you would never notice it. It is, like Coalbrookdale, a real birthplace. Out of film, I stopped at the chemist. He, himself, stood outside his door, on this beautiful, fine day. 'Lovely place', he told me in silvery tones. He was small, pink-faced with powdery white hair; small, shiny hands; shiny feet; and he wore a clean white overall. He reminded me of the great Polish pianist, Pouishnoff, who used to come to Shrewsbury in the war to play Chopin with such stillness and control, you marvelled that so many notes came out in perfect order, so effortlessly. His assistant dealt with the camera while he and I talked about the view and the delights that lay ahead. 'Try Wirksworth', he said, as if it were a good pill.

Wirksworth had everything: a noble church, an old school, a museum, a bakery, alleys – a town without alleys is no town for me – a music shop, the Red Lion Inn, and the Old Lock-up. The latter had a tourist award, I saw, but there was no one in when I called. When I got to the bakery, the lady said 'Try the Old Lock-up.'

'I've tried it', I said.

'Well, I'll give you the number of a lady who used to do bed and break-fast. You can try her.' The lady was full. Try the pub. Reasonable; cost £30; the Old Lock-up was more like a hundred, someone said. To be installed with Elan in this roomy coaching inn was heaven and a load off my mind and off my back. My room had an outer and an inner entrance door. I was like a figure in a double-entry ledger. Accounted for. I had TV, ensuite shower and a splendid bath that rocked you like a pea in a boat. Elan was safe in his shed. I could shed my responsibilities and go breathe the pure Wirksworth air.

'How do you get a piano out', I asked the man at the music shop. It was stuffed with grands – and music shops are not generally very big.

'Easy', he said. 'Just turn it on its side!'

The museum was up an alley, cramped and interesting. It is perfect in scale and scope, dealing as it does with the history of lead mining in the area and illustrating the miners' hard lives, their tools, the constricting con-ditions, laws and customs that governed them. I escaped to the church, where, amazingly, the evening concert by the Derby Concert Orchestra was being rehearsed. Light and sound flooded the building. Splendid banners hung in the aisle, catching and flinging the coloured light first flung by the opulent stained glass. It was vibrant with life. Monuments, which in churches normally sleep, leapt out at you. One was the coffin lid of Betti – one of four priests of Aidan who dwelt here in the eighth century – that was discovered, perfectly preserved, in the mud under the east end of the church that must have taken the place of Betti's and his brothers' Saxon Shrine. The detailed carving in stone may still be seen, raised and mount-ed on a north wall. Next to it is the brass memorial of a child aged 2 years and 4 months. There are memorials to John Toplis, Gent, and to Harry Blackwell, for many years a member of the choir and 'leader in manly sports' who died 24th January 1900, aged 23. Perhaps more poignant still is that of Charles George Marsden, Gunner of the 107th Royal Horse Artillery, altar server, killed El Adem 1946, buried in North Africa. The orchestra and soprano went on rehearsing the Ruhevoll and Sehr Behaglich movements of Mahler's Symphony No 4, bestowing peace and comfort in the elegiac light.

John Toplis, with Arkwright of Cromford, ran a bank 'for the better off' at Wirksworth – and a savings bank (1813) for the less. Retracing my steps to the pub, I found the memorial seat dedicated to Jack Doxey who worked at Arkwrigth's cotton mill and Golconda lead mine and at the limestone quarries after his war service in the RAF, and rose to manage the hosiery factory in Wirksworth. Somewhere, my notes say, I picked up the original spelling which must have been known to Betti: Wyrceswythe.

Back in my room, I studied the inscription over the toilet seat: DO NOT FLUSH CONDOMS, TAMPAX, SANITARY TOWELS ETC. YOU ARE LIABLE FOR BLOCKAGES.

No cowboy riding out of town could have been happier than I was that beautiful morning, Sunday 28th April, the open road before me, the Ecclesbourne railway playing hide-and-seek beside me and only Duffield to do now. No cowboy sung more yearningly: show me the way to go home. But I was not tired; I didn't want to go to bed. I did not want to leave this land of streams and hills. I had felt its healing power, its extraordinary openness. Had the people made the land; had the land made the people? The two processes played together, as the Ecclesbourne stream played and kept company with the railway and the road. 3-ply, as no doubt all those old yarn manufacturers would have recognised. Health is after all a process of knitting: bones, minds and spirits of individuals and communities.

I passed a field in which was a crop which no farmer of my generation would have recognised. It was like a field of young trees blowing in the wind. The farmer dashed into his drive in his Land-rover; dashed out. I could not find anyone to ask about this revolutionary departure from the traditions of English agriculture. I came to Shottle Hall, a guest house, just off the B5923, the Duffield road. 'Excuse me', I asked the elderly gentleman who came to the door, 'but can you tell me what is being grown in the field up the road.' He was sympathetic to my problem. Odd, wasn't it? He used to farm the Home Farm himself.

'Come in', he said, 'I'm by myself now. I'll make a cup of coffee!' That 'now' told me he was probably a widower, running the Hall as a guest house and doing the extensive gardens as a pastime.

'That crop', he said, 'is willow.'

'Whatever for?'

'Well, believe it or not, for energy. Shredded and burnt, it's a profitable alternative fuel.' We gradually found that we had more than a common background in farming.

'I went to the same school as you!' he said.

He had hated the grammar school in Shrewsbury, left early and moved to Derbyshire where he gained a tenancy on the Chatsworth Estate. He had high praise for Deborah, Duchess of Devonshire, on his wife's death from cancer. 'Could he carry on?' he asked her on the 'phone. 'Of course', she boomed down the receiver. He'd never have any money – but what's money? He had a most beautiful garden and went with a lady friend to garden centres in the neighbourhood. He had held quite high positions in the National Farmers' Union; contributed to a booklet on Shottle Hill; preserved old implements... He was, in my eyes, a success – and he knew his crops, though the one we had talked about was very labour-intensive, costly and took about six years to mature!

Duffield: open land frequented by doves.

Maurice and his wife gathered me up, as the Derwent gathers up the Ecclesbourne before wandering off to join the Trent, and made me whole. I like to think of myself as a bit of a hawk, but I am really a dove at heart. Maurice is a thorough-going Derby man. He would sort out my disconnections. Richard Branson would deliver me home intact – I hoped.

Maurice, a retired teacher like me, is a good guide; a benevolent owl, prepared to be patient with one who spends most of his time in the light with his eyes shut. He took me to places that even eighteen-geared Elan could not have reached. Belper was where Jedediah Strutt built his cotton mills. Did he, we wondered, fit out Captain Cook with Derby rib stockings or Nelson with his vest? How many more fine Englishmen clothed themselves in Strutt hose? He took me to see the High Peak railway that I had seen on film at the Wirksworth museum. We talked to a gradely lad who had just qualified to operate 't'engine house up t'track yonder.' It is all that is left of the main line that covered the Derwent valley to Buxton and on to Manchester. We saw the bridge mounted with gun embrasures to ward off Luddites.

Back home in Duffield next day we saw the church – accessible by a tree-lined path which also leads to the river. Back home we were in a glade of peace, seemingly unmarked by Mammon, Smedley, Strutt and Co.

It was Monday morning. The church was open to the light. A class of small children squatted on the chancel steps with their teacher. Maurice was received as a benevolent uncle. As a community worker, one could see that he had successfully bridged the gap between age and youth. We admired the relics of our ancestors – the fragments of Norman stone-work, a corbel table with twelve grotesque heads, an arched recess here, a mediaeval window there. We were in the company of one Anthony Bradshaw whose monument to himself, his two wives and a score of children, he designed and set up in his lifetime. He was the great uncle of John Bradshaw who sat in judgment on Charles 1.

New glass doors had been added to the entrance porch which gave this old-glory church, with its spired tower and many gables, a new-glory look. A perfect way to start the day. And to resume my journey home.

Derbyshire sheep.

What remains of
a pretty dry
stone wall
alongside the
road.

ZOOM EXPRESS

ZOOM it says on the front forks of my new mountain bike; and, on the crossbar, ACTIVE 8. Before long, I mean to add a zero to that.

I have drawn a straight line between Newbury and Shrewsbury – that is Little Ness – making a bee-line map which covers perhaps the best part of England: the Downs, the Cotswolds, the Malverns and the Shropshire hills. It is a rough guide, not to be rigidly adhered to. I will only have to stray from it a little to see such places as Letcombe Bassett, Uffington, Kelmscott, Burford, Broadway, Pershore, Great Whitley, Cleobury Mortimer, Much Wenlock, Haughmond and the country around Nesscliff which I call home. It is the England of King Alfred, William Morris, Edward Elgar, Landland and Roger de Mortimer, Philip Sidney and the young Charles Darwin. Seeing it from the hills, you may see more of its highs than its lows, more of what we have gained than lost – if only super-ficially. It would be foolish not to dawdle. ZOOM will go my camera; ZOOM my memory; but my old legs – as well as the hills – will act as brakes, as they did when I was a boy on my brother's cast-off Coventry Eagle and my mother wondered how I had worn so much shoe-leather out.

The idea is as old as the hills; but in most respects this adventure will be new – as spanking new as the saucy, rather overdone paintwork on my royal blue, red and white CONCEPT mountain bike. And it was so. What was thought to have been lost – to various forms of modern development – is found basically intact; the hills which form the bones of the landscape remain as immediately recognisable as the scarred outlines of the coast, strangely, uniquely familiar.

Old man, new bike; and the bike was the first to fail. We had conquered the downs in the early morning, the sun breaking through banks of cloud on dazzling expanses of oil-seed rape, freshly cultivated fields sparking with flint and hill after hill crested with blossom and foliage – the exercise grounds of race horses, hares, deer, rooks, peewits and skylarks and every creature, like me, that likes to be up and away. We were in Wantage, resting in the Square, King Alfred from the model white statue (the very image of Lord Wantage, one of England's golden youth lost in the Crimean War) looking down on us, rallying us to the cause. Nervously, I put my thumb on Zoom's back tyre. Flat. As if anticipating it, I had noticed a cycle shop only a few yards back. 'No problem', said the man. 'Six pounds.' Thinking that Alfred would have settled for that, I pedalled on, while the going was good.

The pleasures of Buscot lay ahead. You leave the Challows, West and East, and come to Faringdon, wishing that Stanford in the Vale – a mess of quarrying – would live up to its name, then spin downhill through parkland to Buscot. When I walked this way a dozen years ago, I visited the little part-Norman, part-Mediaeval church, forswearing the grandiosity of the mile-long walled estate. To a pilgrim a hermitage is more rewarding than a Great House. This time I was forestalled. A road block had been set up. A hefty black policeman asked me why I had advanced beyond the notice saying ROAD CLOSED. He looked like a young Paul Robeson. I silently admired his white teeth and eyes which revolved under his helmet. He was tall as an ebony grandfather clock.

'I'm trying to get to Lechlade', I stuttered.

'You can't.'

'Why?'

'There's been an incident.'

'What sort of incident?'

'A load of chemicals on the road. Flammable. Road's bin closed twenty-four hours.'

'I can get by.'

'You can't. 'tis dangerous.'

'When will the road re-open? I can't go back again; it's all uphill – and the wind against me.'

'You go back to Faringdon and take the diversion.' He had chided me for taking two steps beyond his ROAD CLOSED sign; but he did not seem to mind that I had ignored the notice about five miles back, just this side of the town.

'I'll have a look round the grounds of the park, which I see are open.'

'Yes', he said. 'Good idea. There might be a road round the back. Or come back here in about two hours.' I reckoned he was on my side, teeth and eyes gleaming with the brightness of his suggestion.

I spent more than two hours trying to find a way round the back, soon beginning to think I had been right twelve years earlier to limit my attention to the church; after all, who would not rather have a Fabergé egg than the whole of St Petersburg? The grounds were open. The car park was open with cars studded about. There were cars left in the drive at the side of the house. An office door was open. Computer screens blinked. Everyone seemed to have gone for lunch. There were no members of   the public, presumably because the road was officially closed. I was alone in this vast expanse of plutocracy. And hating it! I would willingly have paid, not to be admitted but to be allowed to go out! But then I would have encountered my black Cerberus again.

Presently I spied a little man with a van and a step ladder, a handy man, no doubt, with a cloth in his hand. Could he be attempting to clean ALL those Georgian windows?

'Is there a back road to Lechlade, please?'

'Yes, cock. Just go by the front of the house, down the drive to the right – it's a bit round about. You'll see the lake and the cricket field on your left.'

'Thanks!' I didn't see how I could miss a lake and a cricket field.

On my first circuit of these expansive grounds, I passed the lake and the cricket field – and came out on the Faringdon side where my troubles had all begun. On my second, I did the same. I called at the lodge with a notice on a gate saying BULL IN GARDEN. I rang the front door bell. A man – obviously an estate employee – put me right with the aid of a map and assurances that I couldn't miss the farm, so clearly marked. 'It's in the direction of Coleshill, but you don't need to go there. That's out of your way.'

I enquired his name, thanking him cordially.

'Bull', he said, sheepishly.

Another hour later, I was back at the entrance to the park. The road was open. There was no sign barring my way. My ebony clock had called time and gone.

Swapping road blocks for bridges, you come to one of the most appealing on earth: the one over the Thames at Lechlade. It allows a glimpse over the water meadows upstream to the spired perpendicular church with the boats moored like an expectant congregation in between. You see nothing of Lechlade's old mill and coaching houses but plenty of the Trout Inn; and, being on a bicycle, you do not foolishly forego the B road to Kelmscott to the right. Lechlade, proper, can wait.

What, you wonder, riding between fields and hedges bright with yellow hammers and oil-seed rape, is this endlessly flat open Oxfordshire traffic-free haven, disturbed only by the occasional aircraft overhead? Has it lain here, forgotten, since the Middle Ages? Well, practically.

You come to a farm. A pied wagtail pops out from between two loose boards of a barn. A nest, perhaps? KEEP OUT, a notice says. PIC – an affliction of pigs, I guess. No B & B, here! The buildings are all of wood or stone; that silvery-grey limestone which, in the evening light takes on a Samuel Palmer look. Every piece seems to have been placed there by hand with an eye for permanence. Traditional. Elemental. Wood and stone are our time-honoured materials, set to outlast our fashionable PVCs.

You come to the church, which you know is genuine, as you know an oak beam or an old milestone is genuine. The porch, like Buscot's, looks Norman. In part, at least. The door, white with age, is studded with iron – but which is the harder, the wood or the nails? The latch does not budge. Locked, perhaps? You take a look around; you have leisure for a churchyard or two. They tell you more about England than many a museum. On the wall of the cottage adjoining this one are two stone memorials; one to Richard Dufty 'who loved Kelmscott', the other to his mother. You ask at the cottage if you may obtain the key.

'It's open.'

'Oh, I'm sorry.'

'Not at all – but you may have to try harder.'

'I'm sure. Oh, by the way, is there anywhere I can stay?'

'The pub – but that's expensive. You can stay here, if you like.'

That was how I came to know Mrs Richard Dufty – Jean, she said I might call her – and all about Kelmscott, because her husband had been curator of the Manor and in retirement had built a library in the grounds of the cottage, now converted to a guest house, where I might soak myself not only in water from the Thames but also in his legacy. I had fallen into a Utopian dream-world, such as William Morris wrote about in News from Nowhere, except that my arrival in paradise had been brought about entirely peacefully.

I had read News from Nowhere when I was a boy on the farm. It had for me the same open-air appeal as Richard Jefferies', Ruskin's, Jack London's and – if only they had been English! – Walt Whitman's writings. *'O Captain! My Captain! Our fearful trip is done'*, I sang as I put my bike away. *'The prize we sought is won.'*

'What a comedy of errors was yesterday!' I wrote in my diary next morning, after too much reading by artificial light. 'But what a box of delights!' I have not yet got into my stride, I told myself, like any racehorse, peewit, hare, skylark at this early point in the year. Time yet for me to lay my eggs, couple with some Lady Longlegs or hit form for the Derby. Part of the fun, after reading about Morris and the Manor, would be to see it for myself in clear daylight and make my own mind up about this Nowhere from which so much News had come. (And so much else.)

It was not difficult. I was the only person on the scene at about 10 a.m. The place didn't open till eleven. Clive, however, who introduced himself, was already opening the double gates of the entrance and making ready for the day's visitors.

'Have a look around', he said. 'Plenty to see.'

I know a Welshman when I hear one. We established where we both came from. He had been a teacher (maths). Loved working here. 'Put your bag and bike in the shed there. I'll just close it so it looks as if it's locked, see.' I was free to rove, just as William Morris must have often wished he had been free. Not a care in the sky-blue, cherry-blossomed, spring-green, morning-by-the-riverside world. Fantails peered at me from the dovecot; swallows dipped in and out of barn. ('We have owls, too', said Clive.) The brook slid under a lovely little five-arched bridge where no doubt Rossetti fell out (or in) with the local anglers and went off in a huff back to London. Clive was sweeping up the confetti of cherry blossom fallen on the path, minding his own business. What a job! More staff arrived than visitors in that hour.

'Coffee's ready in the restaurant', said one aproned lady, not to be refused.

> *THIS IS THE PICTURE OF THE OLD*
> *HOUSE BY THE THAMES TO WHICH*
> *THE PEOPLE OF THIS STORY WENT*
> *HEREAFTER FOLLOWS THE BOOK ITSELF*
> *WHICH IS CALLED NEWS FROM*
> *NOWHERE OR AN EPOCH OF REST & IS*
> *WRITTEN BY WILLIAM MORRIS*

Most of the guides to the Manor begin with this introduction from Morris's original book. Richard Dufty's set it squarely in the stone-building region of the Cotswolds between Gloucester and Oxfordshire, described it as simple H-plan, 1568, belonging to Richard Turner (died 1600) with some original timber work and fireplaces added to in the next century and a shield of arms granted to Thos Turner, his son, displayed above the main fireplace; noting on the way the special social and artistic connections of Morris who was a writer, socialist, artist, craftsman and manufacturer, resident here as a lessee with some 275 acres with Dante Gabriel Rosetti, Frank Stratridge Ellis and Morris's wife, Jane – all of whose relations he had some difficulty controlling. Eventually he became disenchanted with 'the dear sweet old place', his 'harbour of refuge.' His daughter, Jenny, had epilepsy. An older daughter, May, inherited after her parents' deaths, became the guardian of Jenny, edited her father's works, took up with a landgirl called Lob, actively concerned herself with the social and cultural life of the village till weary of intrusion to the rural peace, died in 1938, leaving Kelmscott Manor in trust to Oxford University. Eventually it passed to the care of the Society of Antiquaries, whose president Richard was.

I had to leave gawping at the wisteria-hung walls of the sparkling straight-up-and-down house and the intriguing whole-stone feeding troughs and drinking bowls (hollowed by hand?) which stood outside the stable block and join the ladies serving refreshments in the barn.

Interiors, I conclude, are for ladies; exteriors for gentlemen. (Free.) Presently I was constrained to buy a ticket and accompany the cognescenti to the house. Yes, I was right. The hands of Jane, May and Jenny were evident here. There were paintings by Rossetti (for which the ladies had modelled) his left-over paint set (more untidy and wasteful than mine) and, among the furnishings, the lumpy old wall-hangings the Turners had left (for warmth) and Morris's own four-poster bed. I tried to imagine how a man of such early originality, energy and taste could bear to sleep in it with such drivel (his own composition) written above him: '*The wind's on the wold and the night is cold and thames runs 'mongst wood and hill but kind and dear is the old house here and my heart is warm midst winter's harm..*'

Mockery will get you nowhere, I told myself. That afternoon I was heading towards Stow on the Wold. Zoom and I declined into Burford, knowing that what comes down must go up. We had too much ahead of us to be bothered with raking over the embers of the Civil War, left lying everywhere hereabouts.

Burford always reminds me of Appleby with almost all its best bits down by the river where many of its finest buildings are, including the church. It is all golden stone mediaeval and stout Georgian facade; all given over to tourists; and quietly dying on its well-shod feet. It suffers from social arterio-sclerosis, like many towns that were once very grand. Its cultural state, like its economic one, must be considerably reduced. I doubt if Rock music ever reached Burford and if any of its tweedy inhabitants like modern music they must have to go to the Cheltenham Festival to hear it. Thus I muttered to myself and Zoom as I climbed the hill out of town in the rain. I was determined to get to Stow – another ten miles – by night.

'It's a bit of a climb at first', someone had warned me, 'but it flattens out.' I knew Stow was the highest town in the Cotswolds and that it had a horse fair, like Appleby, some time in May. It had beer and antiques. It was windy and cold. I had done downs, dales, fells and ridges; but what was a wold? A heath, I guessed. I was still shuddering over Morris's chosen bedtime rhyme: *'the wind's on the wold...'* Thunder rolled round me. The clouds which had massed white all morning now turned dramatically black. Cars started to put their lights on. Lorries gave me less leeway. Everyone was hurrying straight towards Stow, faster than I. A black sky became, like a black eye, luridly yellow and shot with blood. Pedalling like hell, I passed a lonely roadside Inn, stretched out like an Indian longhouse, with clamorous notices urging the travellers to stop and try the hospitality; then, after all the extensions and glass conservatories had petered out, 'YOU'VE MISSED A TREAT!' There were road signs to Shipton-under-Wychwood which seemed more enticing than Stow. Lightning flashed, spelling danger and shortness of life. I must keep going on. Then the thunder broke. The road was suddenly white with cubes of quartz, crunching under tyres and stinging my head, through my hood. I could not see. I made for a small hawthorn hedge – stunted, but all there was – on the wrong side of the road. Wading through rivers of melted hail, I slung Zoom into the ditch and covered myself with a sturdy canopy of ivy, so dense I was almost dry. Zoom's wheels were spinning in the cataract of hail and water that was further flung over us by lorries fighting for every inch of clear road.

'Poor Tom's a-cold', I remember singing cheerlessly, as I attempted to drag Zoom closer to me and into the shelter of the ivy canopy. Never have I thought so well of ivy, though I believe wrens are sometimes glad of it. Even when the storm stopped, the rivers ran on. It was not safe to leave for at least a quarter of an hour. Then, of course, the sun came out; Shipton-under-Wychwood was still beckoning, Maugersley, Oddington,

Daylesford... Ah, here we were at Stow!

The first sign of real life to my thunder-struck eyes was a scattering of obviously gypsy horses, patchy, piebalds splashed with sun, tethered but prancing and drawing attention to themselves on the common just out of town. Why were they restless? Someone – the answer appeared – was looming up on a quad-bike with food. Like-minded I headed for the chip shop, which, I reckoned was sure to be opening soon.

First stop, however, the public conveniences, just on the edge of town where, believe it or not, a tourist map proclaims 'Stow-on-the-Wold where the wind blows cold and the cooks...'It was worse that Morris, and I forgave him – even thanked him for causing me to smile on this near-Apocalyptic day. I found farmhouse bed and breakfast, did the church, missed Vera Norwood who would have told me all about the fair but was out canvassing for the local election, ate my fish and chips and went thankfully dry to my bed.

My most persistent memory of Worcester, disturbing and indelible, is of two schoolboys with 'spooked' umbrellas fooling around on the plinth of Elgar's statue at the cathedral end of the High Street. Elgar himself looked cheesed off, his beaky head bowed to the wind and rain, his frock coat trailing and bedraggled. He had none of that robust, man-of-the-world appearance that I associate with photographs of him, comfortably seated with his Edwardian family and friends (and his dogs) or straining on two feet or two wheels through this demanding Worcester terrain. The man who wrestled with science, talked trade, loved racing and followed form. Besides, some wag had taken a pot shot (purple) at his bum with a paint spray gun.

Worcester is like that – full of contradictions; a rich city living off its purposeful past while struggling to come to terms with its apparently aimless present. More than anywhere else I visited Worcester gave me the impression of being ill at ease with itself. You cannot blame the place, of course; you can only blame the people. Individually, they are like people everywhere. Even the two budding Gene Kellys looked as if they had hearts of gold, or a sense of humour anyway. Then there was Sylvia at the TIC; Linda, my landlady; the lady verger in the cathedral; the bus driver who took me to Broadheath; the girl attendant at the Art Gallery; 'Scallywag' at the theatre; and the several guides who helped me about this most perplexing of ancient and modern citadels of England, lost and found.

Worcester owes its life to the river: and its sickness to the roads which, as spurs of the M5, swoop around it, propelling it into the twenty-first century and strangling it at the same time. The river turns ugly sometimes; but the floods that caused the city founders to build the greater part on the higher, eastern side, also gave the county in which the city is centrally situated its fertility, its mercantile trade, its famous racecourse and its even more famous cricket ground – none of which you see from the Bath Road by which I entered. But you do see the cathedral.

All the traveller needs is a cathedral; sanctuary from England's 'mixed' weather; a coffee shop and choral evensong. Food for the body; food for the soul. But I did need a bed for the night. Where, I wondered was the Tourist Information Centre? It was at the Guildhall, which, however, was so shrouded in scaffolding and further masked by blue (EU regulation) safety netting that I walked past it.

'Where's the cathedral?'

'There!' as if it were obvious. And the TIC? It was tucked away to the side, proclaiming itself on a board to be OPEN.

(The Guildhall was also open, but apart from the entrance hall with its display of portraits of City Fathers, documents of affiliation to Worcester, Massachusetts, and boards with the gilded names of past Freeman of the City – Stanley Baldwin, Winston Churchill Jnr, Elgar, etc. – was minded by two men in blue overalls, one of whom asked the other if he'd like a mug of tea, large or small? 'Yes! Large! and promptly barred the bottom of the stairway leading to the panelled chambers beyond.)

At the TIC a sparky little silver-haired lady with shiny spectacles and purposeful manner examined me as I approached the enquiry desk.

'Just the one night? En suite? Central?', she asked pertinently.

'Near the cathedral, preferably', I said.

In next to no time she had found me The White House, Green Hill Road. ('There is a green hill', I chanted to myself.)

'Mrs Swinford. She's nice. Thirty pounds. Ten minutes from here. I'll mark it on this map which you can take with you.' I wanted to know where the Halifax was. She marked that too. On the strength of money being available, I arranged to stay two nights. I was anxious to 'do' Worcester; and there didn't seem much sense in pedalling north on what was obviously going to be a wet morrow.

Sylvia ('This is Sylvia here, from the TIC...') agreed that I was going to enjoy Worcester and, jolly as a grammar school girl in her gymslip, went on to her next task. And I to Green Hill Road. There were hundreds of school children (students?) swarming in the vast pedestrianised High Street with its replicated bars, take-aways, coffee houses, supermarkets, shopping arcades and malls. None of these young citizens of Worcester seemed to know where Green Hill or even Bath Road was.

'It's off Commandery I think', said a harassed, more mature lady who looked as if she'd been a mother once. 'Ask at the museum. They'll know.' Yes, my map said Commandery; but without my glasses and in the afternoon murk further details were blurred.

THE LAST BATTLE OF THE CIVIL WAR, I read on a plaque outside the museum. I had battles enough! The road seemed familiar; it was the one I had come in on. There, just off Bath Road, was Green Hill Road and, shining in sudden sunlight, at the top of steep steps, the White House and Linda waving, welcoming me. What did she expect, I wondered? Some young thing? She was far from being the grey, lady-in-retirement of the suburbs of my imagining. She showed me my room (high) with its view of the cathedral and I decided to stay two nights.

'That's all right', she said. 'The only other guests are French. Breakfast half past seven?'

'Good morning, Mr Davies!' It was Sylvia in the High, next morning sensing, no doubt, that I was lost between the market, the station and the post office. (The odd thing about Worcester is that, though there are a forest of oddly angled signs sprouting like branches from trees in the street, the main buildings are quite inconspicuous. Only the cathedral and the 'Needle', the old spire of St Andrew's, stands out. And it is as if no one wishes you to see the Art Gallery, which is understandable.)

Sylvia puts me right. 'Have a nice day.'

Well, who could help it. I was going by bus to Broadheath

The bus station at Worcester is subterranean and dark. Between a multitude of glassed-in, zinc-topped shelters, you spy one, number 311, that promises to run to Lower Broadheath at 11.40 a.m. It was my good fortune to fall in with two ladies who knew the area and a bus driver who was a princely gentleman. The ladies were talking about the market and the excellence of the fishmonger there.

'I get my fish from him, always', said the driver, calmly negotiating twists and turns and roundabouts which led us out to St John's Road. 'The nicest part of Worcester', said one lady. 'In the old days.' 'Lovely houses', said the other. (They seemed faded and lumpish to me, like the City Fathers in the Guildhall.) 'He fetches it fresh from the coast every day', continued the bus driver. (He must be exhausted, thought I; but kept quiet.) 'Lovely.'

The ladies were so contented; the driver so rounded and experienced. I felt happy in their close companionship. Was this what made driving a bus in a mad city like Worcester bearable? He was such a peaceable man; so sure of his reflexes. He even had me weighed up. (Old, culture-seeking, not very well off by his dress, but not a tramp – probably some retired estate gardener.) 'How long will you be? About an hour? I'll look out for you in the pub car park. I can pull in there and you'll be safe off the road.'

'Thanks', I said, as I stepped off the bus just outside Elgar's Birthplace (marked). As I said, they don't come better than that, Worcestershire people. Individuals, that is.

I only needed an hour at Broadheath. I wanted primarily to see the cottage which Elgar left as an infant, now simply preserved as a shrine for people like me to enter, observe the pokiness, the old-style furniture, the horned HMV gramophone (at the cutting edge of acoustics then) and the upright piano, like a tawny and yellow two-legged beast, with yellow teeth, backed up against the living room wall. Against the other wall, by the door, a typical round-faced Worcestershire woman sat on the high-backed settle. I joined her. How many days she had sat there I don't know but she was palpably soaking up the atmosphere. She was the attendant.

'Lovely, isn't it', we agreed in harmony. Whatever else there was about the house, there was atmosphere. Here, you could really believe, the young child took his first steps, heard birdsong and listened to the wind which for ever blows through the leaves and through the grown-man's music.

The 'Birthplace Trust' building behind left me cold. Butlin-type architecture and, though free to enter, hard-sell interior. Too much is made of the Engima Variations as if it were the best piece Elgar wrote, unfortunately providing an excuse for predictably weak representation. Why? I retreated to the cottage and its evocative red brick, slate roofed, pig sty-cum-stable-cum-lavatory outside block. A last look at the piano with the fattest legs I have ever seen, a check on the time on the clock – was it a little of Falstaff on record disturbing the settled atmosphere?

'Stay longer, if you would like. I'll take you back to Worcester at two o'clock.'

'Thank you so much', I said, 'but my bus driver will be expecting me.'
He was.

Now, to find the post office (set back obscurely by the station bridge) and
then the Art Gallery (beyond) and then... Well, back to the cathedral,
which was still the only place in Worcester of whose grounding I could really feel sure. The Art Gallery was a disgrace. Confidentially, the girl attendant told me the curator liked to spread a single exhibition throughout the
(several) rooms so that visitors could appreciate it more. Thus, on my visit,
I had to content myself with 'Elipsis', a minimalist expanse of small rec-
tangular blocks speckled with spots and splashes, dots and dabs that any
child could do, given enough pots of paint. 'We have a very fine collection,
really', sighed my confidante. In one side room, however, I found a few
Newlyn artists' work and a small rotunda of Worcester porcelain. The only
other room was stripped bare. Hefty canvases of nineteenth century oils of
what I call the Dark School, lowered over me as I descended the stairs to
go out.

If I have said nothing about the cathedral, that is deliberate. *'Where two or
three are gathered together...'* It was the people en masse in Worcester that
frightened me. How could they, young and old, wander about like sheep all
day long in an apparent trance? (Some may have been tourists, like me.
You can tell a tourist, or any visitor to a town. They have the look of an
observer, of sorts.) These people were observing nothing or no one except
themselves – or each other. School children, in uniform, were coupled
together. All afternoon. Whatever they did in the morning. Students(?) of
the College of Technology, paraded with token rucksacks slung on their
backs but innocent of any sign of a book. It was one endless, depressingly
aimless 'passeggiato'. Boy meets girl, meets boy, meets... It frightens me
because I believe we are breeding a generation that knows not how to use
its time, knows little or nothing about books, or anything that William
Morris or Elgar would have recognised as *'the work of man's hand'*.
Shopping malls are our new temples. The public was invited to view the
architect's 'Prospect of the New Lychgate Mall' near Elgar's stature and,
presumably, where the mediaeval wall and lych gate of the original
monastery used to be. The Rape of Worcester happened about the sixties.

I went to (said) evening service in the cathedral: 'You can manage the steps?' the amiable lady verger enquired. 'Yes, shiny and marble though they be!' I smiled. I sat aloft in the chancel in the choir stalls, away from King John's monstrous marble tomb. Tomorrow night the service would be sung. (Blow in F). More smiles from the verger when I left. She had not had much verging to do.

A banner floated across High Street proclaiming that Great Whitley Operatic Society was performing the Pirates of Penzance at the Swan Theatre there that night. How perfectly English, I thought. How bold and piratical of them to commandeer the theatre like that! Would they be any good? It surprised me that Worcester still had a theatre.

'Two', said an old gentleman canvassing for the election with gloves on. He appeared to be a contemporary of Elgar's, wizened to a single shred of white hair, skimmed-milk eyes behind steel-rimmed glasses a skewed neck and no flesh on any of his small bones. But how animated and informative he was! 'We get good people like Pam Ayres!' He told me where the Swan was. Given time, he would have told me where everything was, but he drove off in his little blue car, only just big enough for his tiny frame. I think – though he was far too much of a gentleman to say – he was a Conservative.

I found Riverside Walk, photographed the bridge and cathedral in the background and fell in with a short-striding, purposeful Worcester man coming from the four-day, rain-spoilt cricket match. He didn't think the Swan was still going: funding withdrawn, typical England! He remembered when Worcester was Worcester.

'Polling Station, see! Is there anything going on?'

'Yes', said a lady in operatic black. 'We're just opening the box office.'

'There you are' he said, as if he'd fixed it especially for me.

There is nothing quite like a spot of G & S to make you realise how good they were, hitting the bull's eye nearly every time and making the mistake of thinking that there may be more to life (or art) in England than what went on in the confines of the Savoy, the Tower of London, rough coastal Cornwall of an English court of law. It was a full house – guaranteed by the mustering of relatives and friends of any decent amateur society. All was well, you knew from the moment the white-haired lath of a conductor, springy as a whippet skipped to the rostrum, swept up arm, kept his baton perpendicular for a moment, then whipped the orchestra into the National

Anthem. Stand to attention! Where did they get those thirteen or fourteen players from? The drummer was especially good. Vintage, like the rest. Only the piccolo, a girl, stood out as a star. Rising, as all stars should be.

The overture over, the curtain rose on a fantastic set. The singers were excellent, individually and in ensemble – and, what is rarer, uniformly and evenly blended and matched. You would have had to be a sour-puss not to enjoy it. The occasional touches of 'amateurism' were all part of the fun. The 'very model of a modern Major General' had it in his blood. The men all had amazingly small, nimble feet. The second act set was as good as the first; the ardour of the performance – they did not overplay anything – even more sustained.

'Oh, yes', said the drummer, whose attention I grabbed in the interval, 'this is as good as I've known – and I've known a few!' All the participants, on stage and off, had this piece in their blood.

A young lad, noticeable for his black hair and shy enthusiasm as well as for the bright letters SCALLYWAG on his black and yellow T-shirt, told me afterwards he always came to their performances. His grandfather had introduced him to the pleasures of G & S.

'What's the Scalliwag about?' I asked.

'Oh, the a-restaurant in Malvern', he said. 'It's gone now. This must be some sort of collector's item, I suppose.'

'Like the performance, tonight', I said.

He lived, I think he said, in St John's Road. Anyway, he went swinging his arms and legs with youthful assurance into the all-tuneful, rainless night. One small piece of England not lost. Yet.

Shropshire is God's own country for me; and I will not bore the reader with too many more descriptions of it. I thought it held no further surprises; but I had not counted on the peregrine. So it is to a secret location in the company of a secret admirer and friend that we go now. (The secrecy, admiration and friendship are all mutual. Fear not.) My identity is clear; but for the purpose of this encounter with the supernatural, we may perhaps call my friend X. He has a small portable telescope (magnification x 70, he says) which, in my eyes, gives him extra-terrestrial powers beyond the other-worldly nature that we were both born with. Poetry is a bond; so is silence; so is a Wordsworthian delight in the simple gifts of nature like rainbows and wild flowers. This Sunday, the fourth of May 2003, the wind sat fair...with noble lustre in our eyes...we stood like greyhounds in the slips, straining at the start... Shakespeare and the King James Bible come most aptly to mind at times like this. This will be comparable to hearing the nightingale, seeing a barn owl or seeing and listening to that most eerily secret visitant, the nightjar. The flesh chills, the hairs stand up on the back of your neck at the thought. And you think of poor old Zacharias struck dumb in the temple for doubting God's word. 'Don't even breathe', my brother used to say to me in the presence of some such wonder, kicking me to good effect.

X set up his telescope on its tripod and invited me to view.
'Just to the right of that young birch tree, see. She's just hatched – you can tell because she's not sitting down flat but raised up a bit... There may be two nestlings with one late egg still to be hatched... She's magnificent!'

'Yes, she's looking out for her mate who may be about to fly in with food for the chicks.' This was my detached attempt to make pure ornithological sense. What I really wanted to say was that she looked like God. The power invested in those feathered limbs, the wings arched like those of the Seraphim, the head haughtily craned, the omnipotent air, the all-seeing eye... left me speechless. And all around, the guano, like whitewash framed the spectacle, high-lighting it like one of Blake's most powerful visions of the Almighty.

'I saw also the Lord sitting upon a throne, high and lifted up, and his train filled the temple. Above it stood the seraphim; each one had six wings; with twain he covered his face, and with twain he covered his feet, and with twain he did fly...'

'The terscel's not going to come', said X.
'Leaving the missus to do all the work', said I, coming down to earth.

'Lords and Commons of England – Consider what nation it is whereof you are and of which you are the governors: a nation not slow and dull, but quick, ingenious and piercing spirit; acute to invent, subtile and sinewy to discourse, not beneath the reach of any point that human capacity can soar to.'

Milton Areopagitica

If I were a latter-day King Alfred the Great I would make Ludlow my capital and Malvern my summer seat. I would call up the spirits of Milton (as close to Ludlow today as when he wrote Comus for performance in the castle there in 1634) and Langland who drew 'in a somer season when soft was the sonne' inspiration for his Vision of Piers Plowman from the Malvern Hills in the fourteenth century. I would not allow either of these great advocates – foremost among castigators of sloth and other sins – to be silenced or forgotten. As it is, I can only glory in what is left of these prizes in the present.

Bowling down to Ludlow – one endless and effortless pleasure along the A49 from Shrewsbury, one soars like the peregrine. The hills on either side seem to have parted like the Red Sea; the woods, streams and fields – one clamorous procession of lambs – cheer you along. Miraculously, the south wind that blew you here has now veered north and is butting you in the back as if to say: 'Go! Go on!' You arrive in Ludlow always in a good mood. The church of St Lawrence presiding over the high town sees to that. You are blessed from the start. A spot of rain only serves to refresh the spirits – and, the sun coming out, the splendour of the place meets the eye like an old painting restored.

That Ludlow is choice cannot be doubted. It is at the confluence of the Rivers Teme and Corve; Roger Montgomery, Earl of Shrewsbury and Arundel arrived in 1085 (rewarded with this prize for his service to the Conqueror) and built his castle to guard these treasured lands, 'beautiful in clear weather and magical in the mist'. Edward IV, the Princes in the Tower, Catherine of Aragon, as a bride, came here. Lucien Bonaparte, brother of Napoleon, spent time in Dinham House in 1810. The splendid Civic Society of Ludlow puts up plaques informing the visitor that, for instance, in Broad Street Admiral of the White James Vashon, once a midshipman, lived at No. 29 from 1742 to 1828. (No. 28 announces: THIS IS NOT A GUEST HOUSE. PLEASE GO TO 28 BELOW THE ARCH.)

I could have found accommodation at the fourteenth century Church Inn, but the twenty-first century Fair was in progress right by the entrance. I dove down Mill Street where, at Manna Oak I could only hear the throb of the turbines drifting faintly away over Roger Montgomery's lands to the south. I would have free access to them on the morrow: Richard's Castle, Ashford Bowdler and Carbonel, Woofferton, Comberton, and Middleton on the Hill... Meanwhile I was intent on enjoying the Fair.

The Fair organisers had commandeered the town, making it impossible for anyone not to become involved. Roger Montgomery, Lucien Bonaparte, Admiral Vashon – not to mention the Salweys, the Davieses and Marmaduke Gwyn of Brecon, whose daughter Sarah married Charles Wesley in 1749 – were all out-manoeuvred. The black-leathered bikers of Birmingham had moved in, Jacks and Jills, amiably 'having a go'. A few terrifying spots of rain fell, driving me into the Castle Tearoom where I studied those travellers from another world at rest. Good-humoured and orderly, they seemed as unbuttoned in their generosity of spirit as they were bursting with bodily bulk. Later, I noticed that they whirled and twirled on the roundabouts as easily as large dancers on a ballroom floor. They had surprisingly small, nimble feet. The men gave a hand and helped the women down when the wurlitzer stopped.

I looked in vain for any youth who looked like one of Housman's Ludlow lads. Was there anyone here among this pale-faced generation that looked as if he could fight a war? One, perhaps. He had working hands, large ears and sandy curls and might have come in from the country. A farm lad, perhaps, who might have known winter and rough weather. Only one small boy with candyfloss did I see; no coconuts; no carousel with its painted horses gently dipping and rising, green, blue, red and gold. There was a Miami Trip in which the passengers were suspended like an inverted convoy of coal trucks derailed in mid-air (the street, a host of onlookers – mostly awestruck parents – oohing and aahing below.) A booth with American machine guns warned contestants that it was dangerous to aim the weapon at anything other than the target. I fled.

The verger at the church was just shutting up but allowed late-comers like me five minutes to reacquaint ourselves with such treasures as the alehouse wife misericord, the Sawley tombs and the 1764 organ provided by the Earl of Powis, MDCCLXIV: just after Handel's time.

'Please hang up', said a prim schoolmarm voice when I tried to 'phone Jean to say I'd be late home the day after tomorrow. (I might with permission try later.) Manna Oak was home for me now. Lovely lemon tea – and yesterday's breakfast ham in a sandwich. Splendid economy! I only needed to make Stow, Burford, Lechlade tomorrow. I must avoid Birdlip. Break through to Tewkesbury and Malvern? The Times World Atlas in the dining room library helped. Malvern it had to be.

I reached Malvern in the late afternoon, just as Dennis Compton Junior was coming home from school, stripped of his blazer and carrying his bat in the way batsmen who have just made a hundred magnificently, proudly and justifiably do. He was perhaps the finest of the many fine images of England I had collected on my way.

Rosendale, my B & B on the Promenade, was a cracker. Zoom rested in the conservatory and I walked out in the evening along the Terrace and down the High where, gasping at the technicolour views to the south, I marvelled at the endless expanse of the plain and the rolling hills beyond. Somewhere down there all my heroes – Masefield, Jefferies and Morris among them – had drawn strength from these hills. All had risen from the ranks. They had all been restless wanderers like me. Elgar, the unelected Honorary President of this Society, was happy to trundle round here on a bike. How levelling and democratic these hills are! And yet, like Malvern itself, how grand!

'What is that lovely line of hills to the south?' I enquired of a couple coming up the High.

'The Malverns, of course', said the grande dame.

'The Cotswolds', said her escort – a former Flying Officer Kite with necktie, blazer and wide handlebar moustache.

Collectors' items abound in Malvern, I'm sure; but the Winter Gardens Malvern Theatres (sic) is not one of them. 'Camille', based on Alexandre Dumas' overdone story of a courtesan was given a workaday performance; but what party atmosphere there was on the stage did not extend to the audience. La Traviata, without the tunes. The Priory, the Art Gallery and all but Somerfield and Waitrose were closed before 6.30 p.m. There were left, however, the hills, the dreamy young cricketer and Rosendale to marvel at. And the morrow would take care of itself.

God had created the world in six days, hadn't he – and rested on the seventh? I could cycle to Shropshire in my seventy-seventh year and back to my home in West Berkshire in seven days – and rest on the eighth. God had never been young. I had had every assistance on my way. He had had none. I was well up to schedule, on my last leg. I had a good bike and the scent of home in my nostrils. I would not palely, yellowy give up. But at 6.20 p.m., I reflected, I was still in Gloucestershire. I had started from Malvern at 8 a.m.; had left Worcestershire trailing behind; by afternoon I had been welcomed into Oxfordshire. It was a bit daunting to see signs to Kelmscott, where I had stayed on my way out, and not be able to turn in. Then at Lechlade you suddenly slip back into Gloucestershire. You know that the length of Oxfordshire still lies ahead. Still, never say die!

I am always so enchanted by the Thames at Lechlade: the old Inns, the church and Shelley's Walk, the humped stone bridge still holding its own and the sleeping boats, moored like ducks to banks white with cowparsley under a new moon – the water still blue with the day... 'Ah!' I slowed, and ran my hand lovingly along the stone arched parapet. It was rough as carborundum. I was still in overdrive. A sudden intake of air, and I was up to speed again, Buscot and Faringdon flashed by. A motor-cyclist headed towards me with show-off lights. A still more swaggering car. I soon reached the quarrying area of Standford-in-the-Vale. I was pedalling wonderfully; quarrying light. I could supply Eddystones around the world. I thought of Paula Radcliffe pounding out the marathon. What did she think about? Me, perhaps.

Wantage, still 10. How far then to the Ridgeway? Alfred had managed that high-shouldered Down without a bike. I saw a sign for Uffington – magic name! Three miles. I could call the whole escapade UFFINGTON (SHROPS) TO UFFINGTON (BERKS) IN FOUR DAYS. It should have been three; but Bank Holiday and the weather had not helped. Then I remembered Uffington had been since the 1974 Heath betrayal filched by Oxfordshire.

More cars showed multiple lights. I began to be squeezed off the road by an increasing number of container lorries lit up like Leviathans of the night. If I saw another sign to Uffington I would take it. Cold, outnumbered and miserable, I wondered what Alfred would have done. Did he ever bother about cold, darkness or wet? Striding about in his Saxon cow-hide cloak.

Somewhere out in the calm grey wastes of Uffington I heard the cuckoo. He seemed to be mocking me. The signposts were three miles, still. Then, after pedalling for half an hour, another two. I peered at Kingston Lisle, Woolstone, Ginge – and White Horse Hill 2. I ruled that out. If I ever reached Uffington I would put up at the pub. I seemed to have pedalled for an hour and lost all the remaining light. I met a girl on a bike without lights, evidently out for a spin. A quarter of an hour later, she passed me on the same road. I was able to ask her where the village was, and was there any B & B.

'Yes', she said, sweetly, reassuringly. 'The white house, straight on. You can't miss it.'

I did. A quarter of an hour after circling the village and marvelling at the great flood-lit church, I saw a youth and his young lady.

'Where's the pub?'

'You've passed it. It's up for sale.'

'Where's the B & B?'

'B & B?' they duetted and squeezed each other.

'Oh, yes, Norton House – by the bus shelter – past the shop – you'll see the sign.'

When I eventually found it, Norton House was in darkness, apparently unoccupied.

I called at a nearby house with light, a see-through porch and large open kitchen where a man was evidently preparing his supper. A kindly man; he opened the door.

'Could I please use your 'phone?'

'Yes, of course. Come in.'

I phoned Jean.

'Where are you?' (She sounded unsurprised.) 'I'll come with the car.' The Good Samaritan and I gave directions.

'Centre of the village. Three-way sign to Kingston Lisle, Kingston Warren and... I'll wait there on the road.'

'She won't be here for a while', said the GS, 'Sit down and have a cup of tea.'

Was I shaking with excitement, fear or horror at the thought of all the trouble I was causing?

I stood by that sign for at least an hour, shuffling my cold feet and listening to the great church clock booming out the quarters – but never, it seemed the hour, so I never really knew the time. I still thought of Alfred and what he might have done, two and a half miles from his Blowing Stone on White Horse Hill. He had only Nature's meagre light – and a candle or two.

Nature's light had by now dwindled to that of the moon and a single star standing over the broad down which separated me from my home. Security lights came on across the road, illuminating the sign and endangering my liberty. I was exposed. I was cold; and, for all my cladding, I felt strangely naked. Cars roared round the intersection of Broad Street and High Street, Uffington. Cars with headlights and tail-lights. Cars with no lights at all. Residents, late home from work or a party. Dare-devils using roundabout Uffington as a race-track. The clock kept tolling the quarters. Dolefully. Lights went on in bedrooms. Lights went off. I might be here all night. What would I do? What would Alf have done?

The security light across the road blazed again, lighting up the sign – and deepening my misery. Someone – the occupant? – was about.
'Is this the centre of the village, please?' I heard Jean's voice.
'Yes', I cried. 'I'm here.' She had been round and round that village, she did not know how many times. I was never so pleased to see her in my life.

A Worcestershire (Friesian) bull with his harem.

Active 8, my new age bike, resting against an Elizabethan Manor House wall at Kelmscott.

CONCLUSION

THERE is no rest for anyone trying to build, or even to reconstruct, England. There are so many components now to handle. 'Handle with care', is all one can say: 'the contents of this package are so fragile – and so precious!' One must not judge harshly or in haste. It is not England's fault that so much has been written that is slanted or biased against her. The fair have always their detractors.

Education is, as always, the key. Readers may have noticed that I have tried not only to portray England but also to set in context certain important figures – important to me, that is – on the way: Bunny Waite and Tony Reid as well as Jethro Tull and Alfred the Great. I dare say I could have dug out some females if time had allowed. Indeed, one could argue that women are essentially constructive whereas men, after boasting about their achievements, set about their neighbours to destroy them. Or men say, 'Look on my works' – from the outside – 'and die!' while women, the home-builders, say 'Come inside!'

Perhaps the psyche of the English male Empire builder was, like that of Ibsen's master builder – and all such individuals – flawed; and therefore only able to produce a flawed masterpiece. We squirm as we shout, not sing, 'Till we have built Jerusalem in England's green and pleasant land'; but no one would dream of criticising Blake's poem or Parry's tune.

'I saw two Englands' is a book by H V Morton, written in 1947 just after the war, in which he cleverly juxtaposes the cosy villages of the Cotswolds and such charmed cities as Oxford or Bath with the England he saw with its nose to the grindstone in the war. Everybody sees different Englands: mostly the Englands they choose to see. There are the Englands of Arthur Mee (The King's England, that was); there are those of Charles Lamb and

159

the vastly different one of his great contemporary William Wordsworth. We have been conditioned by George Orwell in our generation. Even by Jeremy Paxman. There is, of course, a strong strain of egalitarianism in most people's view of England – a natural reaction to the gungho commercialism of most Victorians; but we have not lost our appetite for commercialism, only exchanged one form for another.

No Englishman can be a complete socialist, given the riches he inherits. To be born English should be riches enough. The irony is that capitalism came to this country with the Industrial Revolution: and socialism in the guise of Engels (so nearly English by name) and Marx who formulated their ideas in the slums of Manchester and the Library of the British Museum in London. England, with its vast, enviable resources, needed motive power and the energetic men like Darby, Brunel, Stephenson and Watt to harness it, just as it needed Faraday to harness electricity. Individualists all, you cannot blame the originators of capitalism for the consequences of their brilliant and beneficial inventions.

England was first knitted together by wool, then riveted by iron using rich reserves of coal. The whole miraculous achievement was celebrated and memorialised in that most important of primary resources: stone. It was all consolidated in the eighteenth century. *'If you would see my works, look about you'*, it seems to say.

It is possible to anthropomorphize England in this way; it has the shape of the human figure – the foot stretching out on the Cornish peninsula, the broad girth and buttocks of the Midlands and East Anglia, the strong backbone of the Pennines, the firm shoulders of Yorkshire surmounted on the neck and cowled head of Northumberland, the rugged face of Cumberland looking out on the Atlantic – and this is not to forget the barrel chest of Lancashire.

England's debt to the men of the eighteenth century is enormous. There were many that were mighty – and far more that were meek. Among the mighty one thinks of the Pitts, father and son; Clive, Raffles and Cook; Gray, Goldsmith, Johnson and Sheridan; Constable, Gainsborough and Hogarth; Chippendale and Capability Brown; Cobbett and Tom Paine; Coke, Townshend and Tull; Priestley and Davy; Boulton and Watt; Brindley and Stephenson whose birth date just allows him to be included; Garrick who somehow stands alone; Wesley; Arne and Handel, adopted from Germany, like our monarchy; Steele and Addison whose dates do not quite fit, but whose styles entirely do; Jane Austen, of course; those splendid youngsters Wordsworth and Coleridge; Robert Adam from Scotland who taught us refinement; and Telford (also Scottish) and Brunel, père et fils from France, who together taught us strength.

It is interesting that many of the great originators of industry were Quakers – the Darbys, Cadburys and Rowntrees among them – seeking to improve the welfare of the poor. They came mainly from the Midlands and the North. One feels that England – geologically tilted to the south – kept all its 'grit' up north. The south became 'soft' and corrupt and held the parliamentary power. If the fount of government had been in Matlock, for instance, we might have enjoyed more nonconformity (and honesty). Who can say? One feels sorry for William Pitt the Younger, running all that explosion of industrial wealth and improved agriculture at home as well as the East India and Hudson's Bay Companies abroad while prosecuting wars with the Americans and the French. No wonder he died worn out.

Is it ingratitude that makes the English so like spoilt children quarrelling over too hefty an inheritance; careful to talk about imponderables like the weather, sovereignty or crime; and generally distrustful of foreigners? The English, one is forced to conclude, have a genius for schism; the North-South divide; the Established Church lording it over the Free; the Public and State school systems; the National and Private Health Services; the County House Opera set and those who play Bingo in theatres that have known better days. We have neatly solved – or shelved – the problem of class by pretending that it doesn't exist. For now there are only two classes: those at the top and those at the bottom of the pile.

The delicate question of fox hunting divides the land. One would think it was the most rampant vice on earth. I have lived in the country all my life and only twice come face to face with a hound or huntsman, poor persecuted things – more to be pitied than the laughing scallywag fox! We must WANT something to complain about.

But travel broadens the mind. And when the long trick's over, as Masefield promised himself, a quiet sleep and a sweet dream: that best of all travel, the travel of the mind, where the air is not conditioned, the earth is as virgin as it can be, the water is the pure water of life – and the carriage is FIRST CLASS. And, while one is still sentient, one reflects on the sayings of John Stuart Mill: *'We can never be sure that the opinion we are endeavouring to stifle is a false opinion; and if we were sure, stifling it would be an evil still.'* (On Liberty) *'The liberty of the individual must be thus far limited; He must not make himself a nuisance to other people.'*

Chesterton booms away in the background: *'We only know the last sad squires ride slowly towards the sea,/And a new people takes the land; and still it is not we.'* (Poor foolish squires, who probably never learnt to swim!) The Liberty and Livelihood Brigade will probably prevail, as Benny Rothman's brigade won their right to ramble, because even the 'last legs' of the country are fitter than those of the town. *'We have to learn to love our little platoon place, family, village, before nation'*, said Edmund Burke – a glorious Irishman. So we should not rest our head back on the pillow and compromise but carry on the mental fight.

England: a land you never tire of, though thinking about it keeps you awake at night; a land of such contrasts, diversity and complexity, you wonder it holds together at all.

England: a land where those of us who are lucky enough to live are seldom satisfied; and one on which those who live abroad look back, remembering with affection its hills, streams, woods and fields and say, 'Reckon it's raining there now!'